Who's the Boss?

Lucy.

Who's the Boss?

Enjoy Living with Your Dog Using Ron Pace's Proven Method of Dog Training

by Ron Pace and Vana Ingram

PORTAGE BAY PRESS
SEATTLE, WASHINGTON

Text copyright © 2010 by Ron Pace and Vana Ingram. Instructional photos taken by Russ Carmack, © 2010 by Ron Pace and Vana Ingram; front and back cover photos and dog portraits at the beginning and end of each lesson copyright © 2010 by Bev Sparks (http://dogphotography.com). All rights reserved. No part of this book may be reproduced, stored, introduced into a retrieval system, or otherwise copied in any form without the prior written permission of the publisher, except for brief quotations in reviews or citations.

ISBN-13: 978-0-9843543-0-6
ISBN-10: 0-9843543-0-1

LIMITATION OF LIABILITY / DISCLAIMER OF WARRANTY Used properly, the techniques described in this book can be effective and beneficial, but readers must be aware that dogs that display characteristics such as aggression should be handled with caution. If in doubt, seek the advice of a qualified animal behaviorist or veterinarian.

The publisher and authors make no representations or warranties, including without limitation with respect to the accuracy or completeness of the contents of this book or any particular behavioral result. The publisher and authors specifically disclaim all warranties, expressed, implied and/or statutory, including with limitation, any warranties of merchantability or fitness for a particular purpose. No warranty may be created or extended by sales representatives or written sales materials. In no event shall the publisher or the authors be liable for any damages of any kind, including without limitation, special, incidental, consequential, or indirect damages or damages or losses related to property loss or damage or to physical or other injury either to your dog, yourself, or other animals or individuals.

Portage Bay Press • 4616 25th Avenue NE, Suite 608 • Seattle, Washington 98105
For additional information on Ron Pace or for ordering information, please visit www.canyoncrestk9.com.

Book design: Kevan Atteberry, Seattle, Washington
Cover design: Karen Schober, Seattle, Washington

Printed in the United States of America.

10 9 8 7 6 5 4 3 2 1

I met my wife, Patti, when I was 17; I got my dog Jake when I was 19. Without them both I would not have had the career and life I have enjoyed. I dedicate this book to Patti in appreciation for her support, dedication, love, patience, and prayers throughout this entire adventure.

—Ron Pace

•

In memory of my first dog, Nora, who gave me back my life.

—Vana Ingram

Contents

Foreword 9

Introduction 10

Part 1: Who Is Ron Pace and How Does His Method of Training Work? 13

    Chapter 1: How I Became a Dog Trainer 15

    Chapter 2: The Pace Method of Training 21

    Chapter 3: Training Essentials—You and Your Dog 29

    Chapter 4: Training Components—Your Equipment 35

Part 2: The Training Process 41

    Chapter 5: Use Your Leash To Establish Leadership 43

    Chapter 6: The Heel Exercise 53

    Chapter 7: More Heeling Maneuvers 63

    Chapter 8: "Stay" 69

    Chapter 9: "Come" 77

    Chapter 10: The Finish 83

    Chapter 11: Down and Sit from the Side 89

    Chapter 12: Down and Sit from the Front 99

    Chapter 13: "Don't Touch" 103

    Chapter 14: The Patrol Position 111

    Chapter 15: Off-leash Come and the Chase Game 119

    Chapter 16: Temporary Boundaries 127

    Chapter 17: Permanent Boundaries 135

    Chapter 18: Resisting the Distraction of Another Dog 143

Part 3: Questions and Answers 149

1. If my spouse does the training, will the dog work for me? 150

2. How do I stop my dog's digging? 150

3. How can I make my dog stop chewing my things? 152

4. How can I create an outdoor area for my dog? 153

5. How do I stop my dog's barking? 154

6. What if my dog barks in the car when I'm driving? 156

7. Does it matter if I let my dog get up on the bed? 156

8. How do I keep my dog off the furniture? 157

9. What if my dog jumps on doors? 158

10. What if I want my dog to play with another dog? 159

11. What if we're approached by an unknown dog? 159

12. What do you think about electronic collars? 160

13. What do I do when my dog snatches food from my child? 161

14. How do I handle my dog when guests come to the door? 161

15. My dog begs for food at the table. How do I stop it? 162

16. How do I stop my dog from chasing my cat? 162

17. How do I introduce my dog to a second dog I've adopted? 163

18. Can I teach my dog to stand still? 163

19. What should I teach my child about dogs? 165

20. How do you deal with aggressive dogs? 165

Afterword 169

Acknowledgments 171

Index 172

Foreword

I have been a veterinarian specializing in the practice of emergency medicine and critical care for twenty-four years. Many of the terrible traumas that we see in the course of emergency care are the direct result of an owner's failure to understand how his dog's mind works, and consequently to prevent a tragic accident (such as his dog being hit by a car, jumping off of a parking garage ledge, or being in a dog fight). There are also many people who are afraid of their own dogs, even though they love them and want to provide a great life for them. Some of these dogs will even bite or attack their owners or their owners' neighbors.

In addition to treating any animal injuries that have occurred, we provide counseling for the owners so that similar incidents will not happen again in the future. Part of the counseling involves helping the owners restructure the human–animal bond that they have formed with their pets. To facilitate this change, I refer my clients to Ron Pace so that they can learn the "Pace Method."

The Pace Method of dog training teaches the owner to be the leader in the human–dog relationship, allows the dog to act like a dog, and develops a mutual respect between the owner and the dog. Positive reinforcement for desirable behavior, combined with appropriate correction for undesirable behavior, results in a pleasurable relationship that lasts a lifetime. The Pace Method teaches basic manners and obedience, and then can be focused on the individual needs of the owner and the dog.

Over my years in practice, I have rescued thirty-five dogs (Great Danes, Jack Russell terriers, schnauzers, pit bulls) and have rehabilitated each of them using this training method. All of these dogs have been a pleasure to live with and have been nurtured by Ron's techniques. Many have been re-homed and have provided years of companionship for their new owners.

Ron's method really does work!

Cathy Corrigan, DVM
Chief of Staff, Emerald City Emergency Clinic
Seattle, Washington

Introduction

I was the farthest thing from a "dog person" when I first met Ron Pace. In fact at that time, over twenty years ago, I considered dogs high-maintenance pets with little payback. For animal companionship I preferred a cat—self-cleaning, litter-box using, and not unhappy to hang around the house and sleep all day.

But events in my life led me to a time of worry over security. I suffered from bouts of sleeplessness and fears of being alone in my house. After trying to find comfort in a number of other approaches, such as self-defense training, I decided to try the unthinkable: get a dog.

I knew this dog would have to appear somewhat imposing to serve my purposes, so I figured it might also be imposing to me. That meant my first step had to be to find a trainer who could help me, a total dog novice, communicate with the animal. I also hoped this trainer could teach me how to control my dog in a humane way. Knowing little about dog obedience, I worried that a big dog might not understand anything but brute force—brute force that I imagined could take many negative forms.

By wonderful chance, I was directed to Ron Pace. After receiving positive responses to my questions—Did he help people who knew nothing about dogs? Did he use ways other than hurting the dogs to get them to obey? Did he train people to handle their dogs themselves?—I went to his training facility to meet him.

From the moment I arrived and saw Ron silence a kennel of barking dogs with one command, I was in awe of his "dog connection." When he introduced me to his dog Jake and communicated with him entirely by hand signals, I felt as if I were watching a ballet. It was incredible. Ron's wife, Patti, once told me she thought Ron was a dog in a former life. Maybe so. I do know it was apparent from the moment I met him that he possessed an amazing ability to "read" dogs, knowing instinctually how to reach them.

When it comes to helping owners with their pets though, there's more to consider than an ability to handle dogs. This is where the human part of the equation comes in. As Ron says, "I wish this job were as easy as training dogs but it's not. It's about teaching owners how to communicate with their dogs in a way the dogs understand."

Could he train me? My first dog was a German shepherd I named Nora. Much to my surprise I discovered that I loved working with Nora. As we went through Ron's program I learned not just to teach her to obey, but to "read" her, to anticipate her reactions, to rely on her, and to feel confident and empowered in her presence. I wasn't with the unpredictable, unmanageable animal I had feared; I was with a best friend.

As a beneficiary of his program it's clear to me that Ron has not only developed an effective training method, but has the skills to effectively teach this methodology to others. This ability is what makes him outstanding in the well-populated field of dog-training experts. Dog owners who learn

from him can go back home and communicate with their dogs as well there as on the training field. This is training that truly transfers. This is training that can work for you.

In the years since my first drive out to Ron's training facility, dogs have become a huge part of my life. After volunteering at a local humane society and wanting to improve dogs' chances of becoming permanent family members, I decided to take Ron's Trainer Instructor Course. Using the Pace Method I've been able to help other dog owners as I was helped. And even though my beloved German shepherd, Nora, and her beautiful successor, Brett, are gone, I now have Harper—an insanely happy, energetic dog who brings me much joy. Ever since Ron and Nora came into my life I can't even imagine being without a dog. And I know I owe this incredible gift of animal companionship all to Ron and his remarkable training methods.

In writing this book with him it is my hope to pass on the gift of Ron's wisdom and "dog sense" so that all dog owners can share the joy that comes from really communicating with these wonderful animals.

We are so fortunate to have dogs as our companions. I believe we should make our relationships with them the best they can be.

Vana Ingram
Seattle, Washington

Part I

Who Is Ron Pace and How Does His Method of Training Work?

I have worked under at least fourteen trainers, including such men as Bill Koehler and his son Dick… But never have I known any trainer such as Ron Pace, with his ability to train both people and dogs. His years of research and work have given him an insight into people and dogs that few, if any, of us possess. I am one—as many, many before—who vote him number one dog trainer par excellence.

—*Gaylord Lewis, dog lover and former AKC judge*

Captain.

[CHAPTER 1]

How I Became a Dog Trainer

|||||||||||

MY FIRST DOG WAS AN APRICOT MINIATURE POODLE named "Skip." I remember sleeping on the floor with him the night my family brought him home. I didn't know about such a thing as obedience training then. We just lived with him and he lived with us. My mom would let him out every day and he would travel the neighborhood for an hour or so on his own and come back whenever he wanted.

I also remember something very significant about him. If anyone went into the utility room when Skip was eating he would turn nasty. He had a deep growl and an ugly snarl that seemed to say, "If you come much closer my teeth are going to sink into your leg." You wouldn't even think about trying to get him out from under a bed. If we reached for him in that situation he'd act like a cornered wolf—cowering and snarling. Had I known then what I know now, that behavior would have been corrected. As it was we just learned to live with it and allowed him to control those situations. He died at thirteen after

Ron and Skip.

being hit by a car on one of his independent journeys around the neighborhood. I realize now that Skip and my family could have lived together more compatibly, and even that Skip might not have passed away in that unfortunate manner, had we all had the benefit of dog training.

My next significant experience with dogs occurred when I was in high school. While visiting a friend I saw that her family had a Doberman pinscher in the back yard. I asked if I could take him for a walk, and I walked and walked and walked with that dog. I felt so good with him that I took him home that night and didn't bring him back until the next day. There was something special about that encounter for me, and from that time on I knew that someday I wanted to own a Doberman or a German shepherd.

The opportunity came a few years later, in December of 1976, when I had my own home with a fenced yard and a pickup truck. I knew then that I was ready for a dog, but when I picked up the classifieds there were no Dobermans listed. Of the two breeds I had had in mind only a ten-week-old German shepherd puppy was available. When I got to his owner's place, I paid the breeder $150 for him. He had another puppy there that he said would cost $300, and I remember thinking, "Who would spend $300 on a dog?"

Jake.

On the way home I named my new puppy "Jake," and although I didn't know it at the time, he was about to change my entire life.

Jake and I had lived together only a few months when I saw a television commercial about dog training. By that time I had taught Jake to sit, lie down, roll over, and shake hands, but I knew there had to be more to this so-called "obedience training." When he was five-and-a-half months old I enrolled him in a two-week program of boarding-and-obedience training at the school I had seen advertised. Following their program, I left Jake at their kennel for training. When I came back to get him they took me to a window and I watched from behind the glass while a trainer outside had Jake go through his paces. My dog was Heeling and Staying and Sitting and Downing—all with just hand signals from the trainer. I was really impressed. Then they took me outside and showed me how to do what the trainer had just done. All together I think they gave me about forty-five minutes of instruction on everything Jake had been taught. And that was it. We had just completed their obedience program.

On the way home I ran into one of my friends and couldn't wait to let him know that I'd just gotten my dog back from training school. I said he had to come over so I could show him what Jake knew. As soon as we got to my place I took my dog out in the yard to demonstrate and basically could not get him to do anything. My friend asked, "How much did you pay for that?"

I decided the problem was that I was a little overwhelmed with all the things they'd shown me at the school and that I needed to go back and get more training for myself. The school offered some group classes on Saturdays, so I attended enough to get the drift of their training and later got an invitation to what they called a "fun match"—a competition between some of the other clients and their dogs.

The day of the match was Jake's one-year birthday. It turned out to be a competition between about thirty owners and dogs, and Jake and I won the best "off-leash trained" award, which was a $1,000 scholarship to the school to learn to become a professional dog trainer.

While I waited for my study materials to arrive I decided to do some training on my own. I picked up an adult German shepherd from the Humane Society, did some obedience training with him, and sold him. I soon realized I had a gift for working with dogs and that dog training was what I wanted to do as a career. I built four kennels in my back yard, did some advertising, and started boarding and training dogs.

In 1978 a *Tacoma News Tribune* photographer answered an ad I had in the paper for a Doberman I'd trained and wanted to sell. The photographer had been looking into Dobermans and various training facilities for quite some time. He was really surprised when he saw what I could do with the Doberman, so I asked if he'd like to see my German shepherd Jake work. With flawless precision Jake executed many exercises including push-ups, jumping over my back, weaving in and out of my legs as I walked, and crawling forward and backward—all directed only by hand signal.

Ron and Jake performing.

The photographer was so impressed that he came back with a *Tacoma News Tribune* writer and they put together a feature article about Jake and me.

Jake in the Tacoma News Tribune.

On a Sunday morning soon after I got the paper, and there on the front page was a picture of Jake lying on the hood of my pickup truck. Inside they had a full-page article about us. The writer called him "Jake the Wonder Dog."

Following that publicity, we were booked for various TV appearances—one a prime time segment on *P.M. Magazine.* And when that show was over and they put my phone number on the screen, I had four lines ringing for hours.

After graduating from Western Metro School of Dog Training, I worked for them for a while, and in 1979 I formed a partnership with my best friend and purchased a boarding and training facility.

It wasn't long after that I came to realize that dog training was not so much about teaching dogs as it was about teaching humans how to train dogs. I stopped the boarding-and-training method and designed an intense training program consisting of ten one-on-one lessons for owner and dog: five the first week, Monday thru Friday; three lessons the second week, Monday, Wednesday and Friday; and two the third, Tuesday and Thursday. This scheduling helped the dogs and the owners stay focused and better retain the training information. Once they completed these one-on-one lessons they could come back to a Saturday group class I conducted. The group classes would help them maintain what they'd learned and learn even more.

I've used this approach successfully for over thirty years now. Over that time I've taken the initial training I was taught, effective training I've observed from others,

Group class, circa 1980.

and information I've gained from experience, and incorporated it all into what I believe is the best approach, continually fine-tuning my program to make dog training easier and more effective for my clients and their dogs.

It's my hope that this book will help you better understand how your dog thinks and how you can communicate with him, so you can best enjoy the short period of time we get to spend with man's best friend.

Ron and Jake in the office.

Coco.

[CHAPTER 2]

The Pace Method of Training

IN APPROACHING THE SUBJECT OF DOG TRAINING, I think it's important to realize the reasons that make training such a significant aspect of dog ownership. For the purpose of saving extra words, every time I mention your dog in this book I will refer to your dog as a "he." It's nothing personal; female dogs are just as important.

We Need To Be Able To Communicate with Our Dogs

When my kids were in junior-high school we had an exchange student from Japan in our home for ten days. Natsumi understood no English, and no one in my family knew Japanese. It was very interesting driving home after picking her up. Think about it. Think of how you would ask even a simple question. The communication gap we experienced is like the communi-

Kim and Zeus.

cation gap between a human and a canine, only between man and dog it's a much more difficult gap to cross.

In writing this book I want to show you how to communicate with your dog in a way he can understand without resorting to striking or anger. I believe that in most cases if you desire to have true control over your dog you must establish your leadership in a fair and balanced way. Some of the tools you'll need to do this are: patience, consistency, and a neutral attitude.

Often people call and tell me their dog doesn't really need a lot of training; they only want to learn how to make him stop a certain undesirable behavior. For instance, they only want to learn to "make him stay off the furniture," or "stop jumping on people," or "quit digging in the yard." I tell these people to not expect me to teach them how to stop a specific behavior without first teaching them how to communicate with their dog. This is what training is all about. If you cannot communicate with your dog in a way he can understand, you'll be limited in the activities you can do with him and you'll be frustrated by behaviors you cannot correct.

Dogs Want To Work

There is a feeling of fulfillment, a sense of accomplishment that people achieve in getting some work done before resting at the end of the day. If you've ever been lying around the house for several days at a time, maybe stuck inside sick with the flu, you know the feeling of being stir-crazy. In this respect your dog's situation may not be that different from your own. Some breeds of dogs are not bred to sit around all day. They actually possess a craving for work, and if they don't have a purpose or a job of their own to do, they will find one—like digging, chewing, barking, or other undesirable behaviors.

Champ working for Travis.

Now I'm not suggesting that these dogs need a forty-hour-a-week job; it doesn't take that much to satisfy their desire for a purpose. Obedience training can actually give them the job they need and a chance to accomplish something satisfying.

Dogs Want To Please

Jarod and Rocco.

Dogs are social animals and would like to please humans; they just don't know how. If you've seen a puppy licking someone's hands, or a dog wagging its tail with happiness when being petted or praised, you know how much these animals value human contact. Obedience training gives them the opportunity to learn how to please us and gives us the opportunity to show them how we want to be pleased.

Dogs Are Pack Animals

Understanding natural pack instincts is a critical step in having control over your dog. Dogs are pack animals, and in every pack you will find a leader, also referred to as the "Alpha," or Number One. If you watch a pack of dogs or a litter of puppies you'll notice that they constantly challenge one another for that number-one position in the group. They may compete to get the most food, or to chase or retrieve whatever another dog may want. An alpha puppy may just plain dominate his litter mates by pushing, growling, biting, or even attacking if necessary, to win any fight. This is how the leader of the pack establishes dominance over the rest. The winner, or the most aggressive, will become the leader and will remain in that status until another dog or puppy comes up with enough backbone to show him otherwise.

You should also notice the posturing between dogs. You can see them trying to stand tall, with ears and tail up, to intimidate and dominate one another, and you can see that the one getting intimidated will slink down, his ears and tail drooped in a submissive position. This body language shows dogs' ways of communicating with one another.

Posturing between dogs.

By learning to read your dog's body language you'll have a better understanding of how to train your dog, and you will be able to see how your dog is receiving your directions. You don't want to overcorrect your dog so that he cowers at your command. On the other hand you do want to be able to get his attention so that he is responsive to your direction. In your relationship with your dog you want to become the leader, and obedience training will give you the tools to establish an effective leadership position.

Simon and Cara.

My Approach

The basis of my training stems from my conviction that dogs are pack animals and that every pack has a leader. A confident, well-adjusted dog is one that knows not just who his leader is, but that he can expect consistent and fair direction from that leader.

Use the angle of your leash.

The Pace Method is designed to teach you, your dog's owner, to be that leader. Using your leash and collar, you can show your dog what is expected of him in a fair way without yelling, striking, or anger. You will give one command and then very carefully use your leash to give your dog the opportunity to fall into the correct position If he doesn't, instead of repeating your command you'll repeat your direction, using your leash and your body language over and over until the dog starts to move into the correct position. At that point you can use another tool—your praise—and give your dog a reward for his behavior. In these ways you can teach him how to work for you and how to please you. In the training process this is what I call the "learning phase" for the dog.

As mentioned previously, dogs communicate with one another by posturing, delivering many messages through their body language. They do not sit down and have conversations with one another. For you to repeat a command, such as "Sit, Sit, Sit," in the hope that your dog will suddenly come to speak English and figure out what you want is not providing him with fair direction. With the Pace Method of training we tell, and then we show. That is the way the dog comes to understand what is being asked of him.

For this reason you may notice that there isn't a lot of talking during this training. Commands are given once for things you want your dog to do. For things you do not want your dog to do, a correction is given in a timely, consistent manner, thereby showing your dog that the behavior involved is not wanted.

For example, if your dog jumps on someone and you tell him "Off," does that mean he can jump on people whenever he wants as long as he gets off them when you tell him? Or should you just teach him not to jump in the first place? If you'd prefer that your dog not jump in the first place, then you should agree with my approach to training, which is a very common-sense one. Things your dog is doing that he shouldn't be doing in the first place are things that you should be able to stop without having to tell him anything. **Remember that you are your dog's leader.** If a dog in the pack annoys a more dominant dog, the dominant one will be sure to give a timely correction to the offender. There won't be a conversation between the two of them, there will be an action—be it a snarl or a nip—that will do the talking and say, "What you did is not acceptable."

Your dog, probably like yourself, is more comfortable when he knows what is expected of him and that he can control what will happen by choosing his actions. That doesn't mean a well-trained dog will run the

household. Just the opposite. It means he knows he is expected to obey, and what the consequences are if he doesn't do so. To me obedience means doing something you may or may not want to do, but realize you have to do, and that's the type of obedience we should want from our dogs.

Food-based Training

For this reason I do not think food-based training, which has also been described as "purely positive training," or "clicker training," is a useful technique for teaching your dog true obedience. I *do* use food-based training for training diabetic alert dogs and for puppies under five months of age. I believe that food can be a great motivator to prepare puppies for adult obedience training (which I start at six months).

But once dogs are adult, I don't believe this method of obedience training is appropriate. Throwing treats at your dog for desirable behavior may make him want to perform a specific behavior for the treat, but what happens when he doesn't want the treat? Or when he prefers something else to having the treat? If your dog starts to bolt after your neighbor's cat do you want him to stop when you tell him because you might have food in your hand, or because you're his leader? If the food you have is desirable enough maybe your dog will stay and eat it. Or maybe he'll pause to eat it before he goes after the cat. The question is: will you always have the right treat to motivate him?

Food-based training has received lot of attention recently, and you may have heard of its success with dolphins. Much is made of its foundation in classical conditioning—teaching an animal to respond to a secondary stimulus, or conditioned stimulus, to get a desired behavior. When your dog drools at the sound of his food bowl being readied, the food bowl has become a conditioned stimulus. Your dog isn't drooling because he wants to eat the food bowl, but because he knows that the sound of it banging on the counter means that food is coming soon.

Using classical conditioning, trainers have taught dolphins to perform tricks at the sound of a whistle. The whistle signals to the dolphins that if they perform, a reward—in this case fish—will be thrown to them. In clicker training the cricket-like sound of the clicker is intended to signal to the dog that a reward—in this case a treat—is coming if he performs a desired behavior.

We have few means of communicating with dolphins, so this training method is excellent in getting them to perform. And that is what we are asking of them—a performance. We do not ask dolphins to live with us. We don't expect them to leave their instinctual environment and adapt to the expectations of our world. But we do ask this of dogs.

When we bring dogs into our world, we become members of their pack. You may not look at it that way but your dog does, and pack behavior is what he understands. Have you ever seen a pack of dogs communicate by throwing food at each other and determining which dog to respect based on which dog has the better treat? In his pack a dog's behavior is influenced by both reinforcement and punishment, and he will follow the leader whose leadership he respects. Your dog could care less if

you're the janitor of your company or the CEO, but he cares intensely about who is the leader in his household. That's the person he will obey—and it may or may not be the person holding the treat.

While food-based training may be a good method for teaching your dog tricks, it is not a way to earn compliance by respect. You want your dog to behave appropriately in his environment not because he thinks a reward is coming, but because he knows and understands that he must be obedient to you, his leader.

Board and Train

It follows that you should be the one to train your dog, but some people would like to send their dogs away to be trained by a professional. They either feel that's the better way to get it done, or they just don't want to take the time, or maybe they want to do it that way for both reasons.

I had one client, a professional football player—I'll call him Charlie—who was a very busy guy. He had a nice one-and-a-half-year-old German shepherd named Queen who liked to jump on the sliding glass doors in his house. Charlie didn't like Queen jumping on his clean glass doors, so he wanted to send her to obedience school, where she could be taught to stop that behavior. When he came to me with his problem I explained that teaching his dog to stop jumping on the doors would be simple for me, but he had to understand that just because I taught her to stop jumping on my doors that didn't mean she'd stop jumping on his.

I tried to explain to him that the dog's master—hopefully her owner—must be the one to properly correct the behavior if he expects it to stop. I learned this lesson early myself. Remember the situation I faced with my dog Jake when I brought him home from "being trained?" Most dog trainers could enjoy training dogs, not their owners, and consider that an easier way to make a living. But effective dog training is really about teaching, training, and instructing the human part of the equation.

After I emphasized the importance of his involvement, Charlie said he'd complete the private lesson series with Queen after she'd been trained. I still tried to encourage him to go through the training with her instead of leaving her with me to board and train. For one thing, even if he came back for the lessons, he'd miss out on how she was taught. If he was with her he could learn how to deal with problems as they occurred, from the beginning, instead of waiting to experience situations outside of the training center and not knowing what to do. For another thing, even though he could afford to board and train his dog, why should he spend the money when it wouldn't really give him what he was looking for? In spite of my efforts, Charlie was insistent, and against my better judgment, I agreed.

During the month I had Queen it took two different training sessions with about three or four total corrections and she never jumped on my doors again. So Queen went home and what do you think she did there? She jumped on the glass doors. Because Charlie was never willing to put in the time and effort to learn how to communicate with his dog he ended up selling her to me.

There's a lot of this "I give up!" finality where dogs are concerned and it's very sad for the dogs. Because owners don't know how to correct what may be simple problems they either pen up their dogs, or never take them anywhere, or relinquish them entirely. Dogs can be transferred from new owner to new owner and never find someone who can deal with their issues. This situation is not fair to the dogs, and I don't believe a "board and train" method is the answer. When an owner learns how to be his dog's leader and how to communicate effectively with his dog, he knows how to live compatibly with his pet. That's why dog training to me is actually dog-owner training. I believe if you're not willing to spend a few hours learning to communicate with your companion you should think carefully about getting a dog at all.

If you desire the true dedication I have experienced from the dogs I have owned, along with a trusting relationship of consistent obedience without dependence on food motivators, or luck, or a hope that board and train facilities will somehow transfer their training results to you, read on.

Cinder.

[CHAPTER 3]

Training Essentials— You and Your Dog

IF YOU'VE READ THE PRECEDING CHAPTER you already know how important you are to the training process. No one else can effectively train your dog for you. And the most important thing to remember as you proceed through this program is that *training is a process.* It occurs as a sequence of steps that will lead you to an end result: the ability to communicate effectively with your dog.

I'd like to remind you of those who say they only want to correct a certain behavior their dog exhibits. They only want to stop him from jumping on the counter, taking food out of children's hands, running away when they call him, or whatever it may be. You should not expect to simply correct any one behavior without first teaching your dog what your commands mean and learning how to correct him for failing to follow them.

Your Dog's Readiness for Training

It's important to be sure your dog is of an appropriate age to begin training. As I mentioned in the section on my approach to training, I normally start adult obedience training, which is the training described in this book, when the dog is at least six months old. If your dog is older it's fine, but younger dogs may have trouble paying attention and retaining the material you're trying to teach.

It is also important to realize that all of the training information in this book is offered under the assumption that your dog is physically and mentally healthy and pain free. If you have any doubts about the health of your dog, you should see your veterinarian to rule out any illnesses or other problems that may be affecting your dog's behavior.

Handling Your Dog during the Training Process

As your dog's trainer you should be the one not just to train him, but to feed and exercise him. You should become his sole provider. In other words, while you are going through the training process you should have your dog entirely dependent upon you.

It's also best if you isolate your dog more than normal during this time and avoid having anyone other than immediate family around him. This isolation is especially important if you have an aggression problem with your dog, but in all cases it's preferable. What I usually suggest to my clients is that they avoid taking their dogs out in public and exposing them to additional distractions until they have finished all the private lessons. The main purpose for this restriction is to avoid putting their dogs and themselves in situations they're not ready to handle.

Essentially, if you want to get the most you can from my experience, and from the time and effort you will expend in this endeavor, then follow the process as it is described. Each step builds on the next and will help create a foundation of understanding between you and your dog.

Time Frame

After you have finished working with the triangle exercise described in Chapter 5, you will be ready to start the sequence of training lessons. Ideally you should plan on trying to accomplish the following lessons in five days, at the rate of one lesson per day: the Heel, the Stay, the on-leash Come, the Finish, and the Down from the Side (Chapters 6 through 11). The Sit from the Side (described in Chapter 11) can be saved for another day's lesson.

This time frame will be most advantageous for you as well as for your dog. If that time commitment is not possible, or if you have a problem with a lesson and must work on that lesson for a longer time, then at least try to arrange these first lessons on days that fall as closely together as possible. Once you begin, try to keep to the schedule you set. Not only will your dog learn better if you follow a consistent structure, but you yourself will retain the training better.

When you are comfortable with your results in these first five lessons, you can continue your training with two to three lessons a week—remembering to practice what you've already learned

on the days you are not learning something new. The ten lessons—Heel, Stay, on-leash Come, the Finish, Down and Sit from the Side, Down and Sit from the Front, Don't Touch, off-leash Come, Temporary Boundaries, and Resisting the Distraction of Another Dog—are designed to be completed in a three- to four-week period. During that time you should be working your dog twice a day—either teaching a new lesson or practicing material he's already learned.

Feel free to practice each lesson's training techniques for as long as you like on your own, without your dog. But remember that a lesson with your dog should take no more than *twenty minutes*. After a lesson you can practice what you've learned with him at a later time that same day for ten to fifteen minutes. It's important to keep your dog interested and motivated during the lessons and the practices. You want him to enjoy performing a task and getting praised for his behavior. If you work him too long you will definitely get diminishing returns and not the results you want.

Learning Phase and Correction Phase

As you learn to train your dog you'll be trying something new and then repeating it until you start to see results. Remember there is a "learning" phase for your dog, where you are gently showing him direction until he starts to follow your commands more easily. Once you see that your dog understands what you are teaching him, you can begin the "correction" phase. At that point you can apply correction to get him to perform when you give him a command, so that you won't have to "show" him every time. As you progress through the training you'll be working on one task that is in the learning phase and then working on others that are ready for the correction phase.

For example, when you are teaching your dog the Down, that lesson will be in the "learning phase." But you also want to practice each previous lesson as you go along, so at that point the on-leash Come may be in the "correction phase." If you give the command "Come" and your dog doesn't respond, you would then give a sharper, quicker tug of the leash to correct him.

Praise and Correction

Just as children need structure and boundaries as they grow up, so does your dog. In training your dog, you'll need to use positive reinforcement, or "praise," and negative reinforcement, or "correction." Both are very important in shaping his behavior and in communicating your wishes to him. Do not expect your dog to behave as you wish unless you've corrected him when he makes a mistake. And just as you work for money, or another form of reinforcement, your dog works for praise. Do not expect him to work for free.

On the other hand, do not expect your dog to be motivated to work for you if he's getting everything free from your family and the other people he encounters. You want him to look to you for his reward, for his "paycheck." That's the reason I say, "As your dog's trainer you should be the one not

just to train him, but to feed and exercise him. You should become his sole provider." For best results while you are going through the training process you should have your dog entirely dependent upon you.

There are two types of praise you will use to reward your dog—verbal praise and hand praise.

Verbal Praise

You use verbal praise to reward your dog when he is in the act of doing a task properly—either when he's nearby you or when he's out of your reach—by saying the phrase, "Good boy," or "Good girl." The tone of voice you use when you praise your dog is crucial. Women tend to excite, or encourage, a dog more easily than men because they can give a higher pitch to their words. If you don't have a high pitch in your voice you can learn to use a drawn-out whisper-like sound that dogs also seem to like.

When you're praising your dog you also need to notice if he is responding to your praise. Look for a sign from his body such as a little tail wag, movement of his ears, or anything that shows you he's acknowledging what you're doing. If he's not responding, then you're not satisfying his need—to please you or to accomplish something—and you will not get the results you should expect.

Hand Praise

Hand praise is patting or stroking your dog when he has completed a task properly. You should vary the way you stroke your dog, depending upon his temperament. For instance if you have a dog that's high strung and gets easily excited, slow, calming strokes will help keep him calm. On the other hand if your dog is too laid back or slow moving, using faster strokes and providing a more hyped-up level of praise may help him get more interested in what you're asking of him.

"Rubbing him up."

Before you start training, you can see how your dog likes the type of hand praise you're giving him by stroking or rubbing him strongly and rapidly—what I like to call "rubbing him up"—as you tell him, "Good boy, good boy." Praising him verbally while you're rubbing him up will condition him to associate your verbal praise with a positive feeling and will help you when your dog is out of reach. If you do this conditioning well he will feel just as good hearing your verbal praise from a distance as he would feeling your hand praise when he's near you.

A Pat on the Back

There's a difference between praise, which is a reward, and a pat on the back, which gives your dog another useful message. After you've made a correction you don't want to tell your dog "Good boy," since the behavior you corrected is not behavior you want to reward. Instead you should give him a pat on the back, which will "balance" your correction.

> *Pat your dog on the back often. This gesture lets your dog know that you still like him, that you're not angry even though he may have done something you corrected, and most importantly, that you hold no grudge against him.*

Balancing Your Praise and Correction

Achieving balance is extremely valuable in your training endeavors. If you overcorrect or over-praise your dog it will hinder your speed in progressing through training and could even harm your relationship with your dog.

As an example, my new pup Jay is much more sensitive than my last dog, Jet. Jet was Jay's grandfather, but what a huge difference! Jet was what I call a very "hard" dog, while Jay is more on the "soft" side like my first dog Jake. Even though he's a German shepherd, Jay wants to please the way a golden retriever does, which is good. But on the other hand he's too sensitive to correction. That means it doesn't take much to correct him, and if you overcorrect—make your corrections too hard, too sharp—it takes time to get back the "balance." If you overcorrect you need to undercorrect for a while to build confidence in your dog. That's what I mean by achieving "balance." If I've overcorrected Jay I take him up to my mountain cabin for a week and hang out with him. This might seem a little extreme, so I don't tell my wife my reason. She thinks I'm up there to work on this book.

Riley.

[CHAPTER 4]

Training Components—
Your Equipment

||||||||||

JUST AS USING THE PROPER EQUIPMENT for construction makes building a house easier, using the proper equipment in dog training makes your training efforts much more successful. The main tools you need for training your dog are a six-foot-long nylon leash and a metal choke collar.

Two thicknesses of nylon leashes and metal chains.

Nylon Leash

Your leash is a critically important tool in communicating with your dog. It provides you the means to let your dog know what you are asking of him.

I prefer to use a nylon leash, because the material allows for a comfortable grip and easy movement of your hands in sliding down the leash quickly. You need to have this ease of movement to make your corrections as quickly and effectively as possible, which is very important in the training technique I'm teaching you. Nylon is also strong and, unlike leather, it doesn't stretch.

The six-foot length is important because you want your dog to learn to respect the length of the leash and to know how far he is expected to be from you. People often purchase retractable leashes in a misguided effort to be "kind" to their dogs and to give them extra space. They not only give up control with this type of leash, they also send a confusing message to the dog, because his boundaries are constantly changing. If you want to discourage pulling and be able to correct your dog effectively, you need to work with a six-foot leash. If you already have a retractable leash you can save it for later—after building a training foundation with your dog, you could possibly use it for exercising with him later.

The thickness and width of your leash can vary depending on the size of your dog. For medium-to-large dogs the leash should be one-inch-wide nylon made of single-ply parachute webbing, with a one-inch clip at the end. For smaller dogs or puppies, the leash can be of half-inch-wide nylon. If you cannot find appropriate leashes at pet supply stores, you can make one with a sewing machine. Awning supplies stores carry one-inch webbing, and marine supply stores have one-inch brass clips.

One-inch brass clip.

Holding Your Leash

Hold your leash by placing the loop around your thumb and closing your remaining fingers around the loop, "locking" the leash in your hand with this grip. You can easily transfer the leash from hand to hand by simply moving the loop from thumb to thumb and continuing to lock the leash in the hand that's holding it. Use your other hand to control the amount of slack that lies between you and your dog.

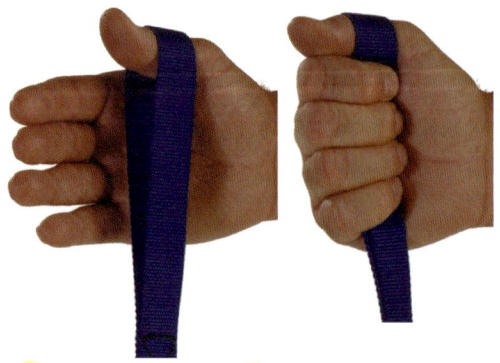

Place the loop of the leash over your thumb… *…and close your fingers around the loop.*

Introducing Your Dog to the Leash and Collar

Before you put a choke collar on your dog he should already be comfortable with walking on-leash while wearing a nylon collar. You can start accustoming him to this activity from the time he is six weeks old.

To introduce your dog to a leash and nylon collar, get the widest nylon collar that will fit snugly around his neck and let him wear it around for a day or two.

After he's worn the collar for this amount of time, you should set up a situation that will help you introduce him to a leash. Attach your leash to his collar and follow your dog around. Let him do the leading while you do the following, always being sure to keep the leash taut.

You can do this by taking him somewhere that he'd find interesting and would want to explore. Another approach would be to have someone he wants to follow entice him so that he'll head off in his or her direction. If your dog is a puppy you might have the person he's following bait him with food every so often.

Keep the leash taut as you let your dog lead.

Hold your leash with the thumb of one hand in the loop of the leash while you use the other hand to pick up or let out as much slack as you need to keep the leash taut. Keep the line of your leash aimed toward your dog's tail and do not try to lead him or to drag him! Also be careful that you don't allow the leash to move around to the front of your dog's mouth. You don't want to encourage him to grab it.

With the leash held in one hand, use the other to control the slack.

The idea of this exercise is to have your dog pull ahead without worrying about the slight pressure of the leash behind him. Young puppies may only tolerate this activity for about five minutes at a time in the beginning. Remember when doing this to follow your dog and not to try to lead until you believe he is very comfortable with the tension of the leash on his neck. You'll want to repeat this experience at least twice a day for a week until your dog is comfortable pulling you around. Then you can start leading him in your direction by giving slight tugs on the leash and encouraging him to go with you.

If you have made the collar-leash introduction smoothly you'll find that when you move to placing a properly fitted choke collar on your dog he will accept it easily and will not panic and have a negative experience.

Choke Chain

The next tool you need is a choke chain, or choke collar. Now I realize that the name "choke collar" doesn't sound good. I also know that if you put one around my neck and got away with giving it a good jerk—the first time that happened would be the last time. But we are members of the human species, and the collars are meant to be worn by the canine species. Dogs have very strong necks, far stronger than, say, the mid-point of your leg between your knee and your hip. In fact dogs' necks are so strong that they could possibly pull a person up and down the street with the chain in "full choke" mode, or tightened as much as possible. Seeing this happen with a dog would illustrate the fact that choke chains are not meant to be used by people who don't know how to use them! That's why you're reading this book: so you can learn how to use training tools properly and so you can teach your dog not to choke himself and/or pull you all over the neighborhood.

Selecting a Chain

In selecting a choke chain it's important to choose a metal chain that has the proper length, link, and weight. The chain should be of a good quality metal, welded so that it doesn't have a tendency to break, and the links should be very smooth so that the chain slides easily. The choke collar is intended to have smooth links so that it can be tightened and released (or loosened) quickly.

In selecting a size, you should get a chain that is approximately three inches longer than the circumference of your dog's neck. Of course this measurement will not apply to very small dogs, like Chihuahuas; for them you should consider a size that will enable you to fit your fingers, up to the middle knuckles, beneath the chain when it is around the dog's neck. For any dog, if the chain is sized properly it should fit snugly without a loop of extra slack drooping down below the dog's neck. With a good fit you should be able to just slip your hand (or for smaller dogs, your fingers) between the collar and your dog's neck when he is wearing the chain.

The weight of the links is also important. A miniature poodle, for example, could wear a twelve-inch medium chain, while a good-sized cocker spaniel might take a sixteen-inch heavy or an eighteen-inch extra-heavy. Once you have a dog that needs an eighteen-inch or larger chain, the links need to be extra-heavy.

When Should Your Dog Wear His Choke Chain?

Your dog should be wearing his chain twenty-four hours a day, seven days a week. If your dog is with you and you don't have a collar on him, you can't communicate with him.

I know that many of you have heard that you should not keep a choke chain on your dog all the time. I agree with this advice only if your dog's collar is too long and hanging off his neck so that it can readily get caught on something. Or if you are confining your dog for long periods in some makeshift kennel that has wires that stick out and could catch on his chain.

Putting on the Chain

To put the choke chain on your dog, tuck the middle links through one of the rings and pull the rest of the chain through the ring. Face your dog and hold the chain so that it forms the letter "P" with

the free ring (the ring to which you will attach your leash) hanging down, then place it over his head. When the chain is placed on your dog in this manner and you are facing him, it should lock when you slide it in a clockwise direction around his neck, and simply slide when you take it in a counterclockwise motion.

Prong Collar

Different sizes of prong collars.

At some point, depending on your dog, you may need what is called a prong collar or pinch collar. This is a metal collar with prongs protruding from the chain.

In terms of producing pain, this collar looks far worse than it is. If you put it around your leg above your knee and tighten and release it you will see that the effect it produces doesn't feel as uncomfortable you might expect.

Form the letter "P" as you face your dog.

The prong collar can be a very effective tool for dogs that have a high tolerance to pain. The idea is not to use the collar to hurt your dog, but to use it to get his attention and gain the responsiveness you want when you're not able to accomplish that with the choke collar.

I can use the following example to show you what I mean. When I was younger I once traded a dog for a horse. The horse was a mustang, saddle bred, and if you know horses you know that mustangs like to run and run. I rode that horse home, which was five miles away, and boy, was that a rough ride. It was probably similar to the feeling you'd have if your dog pulled you down a road as fast and as far as he wanted to go without stopping. I didn't know when I took that horse that the equipment that came with him was a soft bit, and that there was such a thing as a hard bit, intended for tougher horses such as he was. A hard bit would have been a very valuable tool for me then, and would definitely have helped me control him and made for a safer ride home.

The prong collar around your dog's neck feels as it would around your thigh.

The prong collar is a tool that can be used in a similar way with your dog. It's NOT intended to be a band-aid, or something kept on your dog all the time to keep him from pulling. It's intended to be used as a tool to condition your dog, to slow down a determined, headstrong animal, and to help you control him in a way that will show him what you expect. You can go back to using your regular choke chain after your dog is conditioned enough or understands that pulling on the leash is not going to be accepted.

Part 2

The Training Process

By the time the classes were over, I had learned more than I ever thought I would. By helping me learn how to teach him, by teaching me, my dog has become all I could want in a dog.

—*R. Smith*

When I started, I thought that Ginny was going to get most of the training, but I was wrong. The program really focused on teaching *me* the correct way to handle my dog and to make the subtle corrections that she quickly learned to follow. Ginny's behavior has improved tremendously and she is a much happier, more responsive dog.

—*L. Wright*

Simon.

[CHAPTER 5]

Use Your Leash to Establish Leadership

|||||||||||

WHEN MOST BEGINNING STUDENTS ARRIVE at my facility they are in the habit of allowing their dogs to dictate where they will go. This first training session should play a very strong role in reversing that situation. You need to be your dog's leader. You lead. Your dog follows. Wherever you go, from this point forward, consider yourself as the leader.

Using Your Leash Effectively

To ensure that you are the leader you need to take full advantage of your leash as a tool. Remember to hold the leash so that the loop is over your thumb and in the "locked position." Do not put your leash over your hand—in other words, do not put your fingers or wrist through the loop. This position could result in the leash slipping too easily from your hand if your dog decides to make a sudden movement, or in an injury to you if your dog suddenly bolts and drags you after him. When you hold your leash incorrectly you are also prevented from making effective corrections with it.

If you can keep your hands close to your body, near hip level, you'll allow yourself adequate space to "release" the leash (that is, let out the slack) and snap it sharply when you need to make a correction. You'll also find it far easier to handle a larger dog if you keep your arms closer to your body, or in other words, if you keep them closer to your center of gravity. This is an especially helpful concept for anyone who doesn't have a lot of upper body strength.

Hold your leash close to your hip when the leash is fully extended.

Correcting Your Dog if He Bites at the Leash

If your dog bites at the leash, pull it straight up and out of his mouth, then immediately release the tension and give him the opportunity to make his mistake again.

If he bites again, pull the leash straight up again. After the negative experience of having the leash quickly snatched from his mouth, your dog should be reluctant to grab it again.

When correcting your dog your timing is everything. Just as his teeth are reaching his target (the leash), quickly jerk up and release so the leash runs through his teeth. The idea is to have the leash run through his mouth and be released before he can grab hold of it. If you allow a 'tug of war" game to start, you will lose.

If you have a very determined dog, though, and he still grabs on solidly after you've tried this technique, you may need to make your correction stronger. Once your dog has grabbed the leash and has it in his mouth, let him keep that part in his mouth. Take the remaining part of the leash and wrap it around the back of his head, back into his mouth, and back around his head again. If this is done correctly, your dog should then have two straps of leash in his mouth and two straps of leash around the back of his head. Keep pressure at the back of his head for about thirty seconds or until you can see he's very uncomfortable with the leash in his mouth and wants it out. At that point release your hold, let the leash hang loose, and wait to see if he'll grab at it again. If you've done your correction effectively—that is, held long enough for him to really want that leash out of his mouth—your dog's leash-biting should come to an end. If it doesn't, you must repeat the correction. Remember to be consistent, and remember: your leash is your tool; it's not your dog's plaything.

Correcting Your Dog for Jumping Up on You

If your dog tends to jump up on you, get ready to correct him by first attaching your leash to his choke chain. Remember: your leash is your tool, and it can really help you in this situation.

As your dog jumps, and before he's actually placed his front paws on you, slide your free hand—the hand that's not locked in the leash loop—out to your side. If you do this in a sharp motion you should be able to give

Slide your free hand out to the side.

Give the collar a quick snap.

your dog's collar a quick snap and release, and he should find himself landing off to the side, instead of on you.

After you've made this correction, and your dog is again standing with all four paws on the ground, give him a pat on the back. As mentioned earlier, this gesture "balances the correction." It lets the dog know that you're not mad at him; it's just that a certain behavior of his (jumping on you) will always elicit a certain reaction from you (a snap off to the side). Balancing the correction is like saying to him, "Hey, it's nothing personal. It's just that when you do this, my arm suddenly does this." You'll need to repeat this correction every time he jumps on you so that he's unable to complete his desired action of putting his front paws on you.

Your dog should land off to your side.

It will take some practice for you to make your correction a snap of the collar, rather than a jerk of the dog, but the proper correction should discourage him from this activity.

If you have a persistently jumping dog and this correction doesn't seem to be enough to stop him, catch him in the air as he jumps up, by holding him up tightly with your leash. Hold him up for about a second, and then give a sharp snap downward to one side.

Be sure to make that last downward movement a *snap,* not a *pull.*

Catch your dog as he jumps, and hold him up.

Give a sharp snap downward.

If your dog is so determined that he jumps on you from behind, immediately turn around as soon as he does it and make that same correction—holding him up for a second and then giving his collar a sharp snap downward.

If your dog is too fast for you and manages to jump up, touch you, and land on the ground before you can stop him, you must re-create his mistake. Lift him back up where he was in the air before he touched you, and then quickly make your downward correction. If you want to successfully correct his jumping behavior you must not let him get away with it, even if that means you must re-create his mistake every time he does it. If you let him get away with his mistake he won't be discouraged from jumping, he'll only be confused.

Remember: Never let him jump on you without a correction!

Jumping on Others

One situation you might anticipate is that your dog will jump on other members of the family or guests as he greets them or tries to get their attention. In this case you want to make the same correction we described above—a sharp downward snap—but you'll be making the snap out to the side, away from the person the dog is jumping on. If he jumps up on someone and then gets away before you can make the correction, you need to recreate his mistake. Take him back up to the person he jumped on, lift him up to the place where he made his mistake, and then give the sharp snap downward and off to the side. You don't have to pull him up onto the person; just close to the person. Again, just as with jumping on you, you must not let your dog get away with this behavior without receiving a correction.

It's also worth noting that the correction for jumping, as it's described, depends on the use of your leash. If you take your leash off and your dog jumps without receiving a correction, you'll ruin the conditioning you've been working to establish.

You could try to catch your dog by the collar and make that same downward snap, but it will be more difficult. A better approach would be to anticipate the jumping behavior before it occurs and be ready for it by attaching your leash to your dog ahead of time.

Make Your Corrections as Effective as Possible

When you make your corrections, be sure to stand up straight. Avoid eye contact with your dog unless you're making the correction. By this I mean don't let him know that you're watching him. In this way he'll know that his undesirable action caused your attention and that everything's okay when there is no eye contact.

Timing is very important in making *any* correction, and the time you finish a correction is as important as the time you begin it. For example, in making the correction just described, stop your

eye contact as your dog is falling downward. You want to change your focus at that point so that he'll know then that the correction is over and everything is fine.

> Many people continue to look at their dogs after they've corrected them—be it for jumping or other undesirable behaviors. To the dog this continued focus means he is still being corrected. In all your training you want to make it very clear to the dog: this was the undesirable behavior, this was the correction, now it's over.

Walking "on Break"

When your dog is on-leash and simply walking with you, he is "on break" or, as you might say in military terms, he's "at ease." While walking on Break he's allowed all six feet of your leash and can move completely around you in a 360-degree range. It's as though you hooked him up to a pole and he could circle completely around it without getting tangled up.

As you hold your leash with one thumb locked in the loop, you can transfer it from one thumb to the other as your dog moves from one side to another. If your dog wants to walk around you, you can transfer your leash from thumb to thumb behind your back.

On Break your dog can go to your right, your left, around you, and also come close to you or move away. As he comes close you need to take up the slack of the leash with your other hand (the one not holding the leash) so that his legs don't become tangled. If he wants to move away from you, you need to release the slack and let him have access to the length of the leash.

When walking on Break, use both hands to manage your leash.

Don't follow your dog with a loose leash. You want to keep the leash comfortably taut, but without restricting your dog or preventing him from taking the full length of the leash. It's as if you were holding a retractable leash that you had to maneuver manually.

The "Break" Command

When you have your dog on the leash and you give your dog the Break command, it means that he's free to move about as he wishes, for the six-foot length of his leash. This command will release the dog from any position, such as Sit, that you place him in. Releasing the dog, or Breaking him is just as important as teaching him to obey your commands to Sit, Heel, or whatever else you may ask of him! It is necessary for the dog to know that he has fulfilled your request and that you will be releasing him, or telling him he can be "at ease" after he has performed. You do not want to have your dog determine when he should leave a Sit, Stay, or Down. You are the leader, and as such you should let him know when he has fulfilled his assignment.

It's also worth mentioning here that you do not want to set your dog up for failure by requiring more of him than could reasonably be expected—such as holding a Sit–Stay for too long—but we will get back to what you should be able to expect in future lessons.

To teach your dog what the Break command means, say "Break," and then move backward (not forward!) away from the dog. If your dog doesn't move, give a light tug on the leash from about four feet away. This would be about the length of the leash if you were holding it in the Heel position. With this tug you want to get your dog to rise from a sitting position. As soon as he does, praise him.

On Break he can sniff the ground, stand, sit, move around you, or lie down, as long as he stays within the six-foot radius of the leash and doesn't pull on the leash or jump on you.

Correcting Your Dog when He Pulls Too Hard on the Leash

Handling your dog as he's walking on Break may be fine, but what happens if your dog wants more than the six feet of leash you're allowing him? What happens if he wants those six feet plus the two feet of your arm plus, say, whatever he can get by pulling you as far or as long as he likes?

The Brick Wall Effect

To answer that question I'll ask another: What would happen if you fastened one end of your leash to a brick wall, the other end to your dog's choke chain, and your dog decided to take off heading straight away from the brick wall?

If the leash and collar are strong enough, he'll probably find himself stopping pretty suddenly and it's likely he won't try that again. Can you see that image? Well, you need to be that brick wall. If your dog comes to the end of his leash and wants to go farther, he will "hit a brick wall." He can go no farther and he cannot pull your arms away from your body. You do not go forward with your dog!

Leash Correction for Pulling

When you attach the leash to your dog he's likely to react in one of two ways. One is that he may take off running away from you to head in whatever direction he wants. If that should happen you want to ready yourself to employ the "brick wall effect." Stand firm. Let him hit the end of the leash, then release the tension so that he will continue to hit the end until he quits trying.

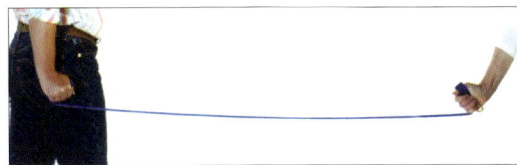
Leash pulled tight.

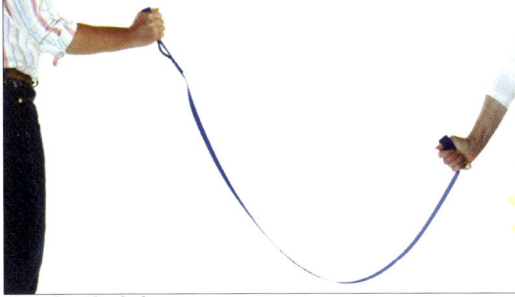
Releasing the slack.

Making a snap of the dog's chain.

But he may also work his way to the end of the six foot leash and *then* begin to pull harder and harder. In this case be sure to keep your hand close to your hip so that once you determine that he's pulling too hard, you can release your slack and make a sharp snap of the dog's chain.

If your dog is pulling on his leash you want to correct him by *snapping* the leash, not by *pulling* back on the leash. Think of the motion involved in snapping a towel against something, or some unfortunate someone. This is the quick snap you want to make with your leash, and the quickness of the snap is what makes this correction effective. You want your correction to snap, or tighten and release, the dog's collar, not the dog. Put another way, you ideally want to tighten and then suddenly release the collar without physically moving the dog's head. Practice by holding your leash properly with thumb in loop and have a helper hold the clip of the leash. With your hand at your hip, reach out from your hip about a foot and quickly snap the clip without moving your helper's hand.

Remember that you want to make your correction only when your dog has reached his limit of six feet of leash and still continues to pull hard. Don't correct him for pulling before he reaches the end of six feet. This means you don't correct him from a three- or four-foot length of leash. When your dog is walking on Break you are promising him the full six-foot length of his leash. If you correct him from a shorter distance it will be confusing to him.

> *Most students also make the mistake of snapping their leash as soon as it gets tight instead of waiting until the dog is pulling too hard. Remember that your dog should learn that he will be corrected not for being at the end of his leash, but only for trying to pull too hard. You should expect some pull on your leash, but should not feel that the dog's pull is making it difficult for you to keep your hand close to your body. If this is the case then the pull is too strong and your dog deserves a correction.*

When you feel your dog has come to respect the six-foot length of the leash and doesn't pull when you are just standing still, then you are ready to start the triangle exercise described in the next section.

The Triangle Exercise

Before you teach your dog to Heel, you must show him that you want him to follow your lead, and this is where the triangle exercise comes in.

Find three points to form a triangle.

To begin this exercise you'll first need to find a training area free from distractions. Actually for all the lessons described in this book you should have such a place. It could be your back yard or a park area that's not actively utilized.

> *The important thing to look for is a space that will allow you to work with your dog where he can focus his attention on you—not on other dogs, people, traffic, or other distractions.*

Once you've found your training area, locate three focal points to make a triangle. For example, a tree, a bush, and a corner of your house could serve as triangle points. Imagine a straight line running from point to point so that you can "see" the triangle. Now you're ready to begin. With your dog on Break, start walking to one of the three points. If your dog starts to run in front of you, turn and go toward another point. If your dog doesn't readjust himself and come with you, he'll find himself at the end of the leash and experience the "brick wall effect." It's a similar situation to the one when you were standing still and he took off. The difference is that now you are a "moving brick wall." He must go with the leash—and you—or find himself in an uncomfortable position.

As you walk from point to point, make sure to let your leash run out as he goes away from you, and be sure to take up the slack, or bring it in, as he comes close. Transfer the leash from hand to hand behind your back as he travels around you. In choosing which point of the triangle will be your target, always move in a direction that is opposite from the one your dog wants to take. Don't put yourself in the position of following your dog—he should follow you. Keep moving at a steady pace, from point to point, repeating the change of direction until you see that your dog is paying attention and going with you to avoid being caught by that brick wall effect. Start by making slow turns, and then make faster turns as he gets better at following you. Or when you see him take his eyes off you. Verbally praise him when you see that he's making the turn or shifting direction with you, and stiffen up like a wall when he ignores your turn. Your movements and your praise should encourage him to keep his eyes on you so that he receives praise rather than correction.

If your dog is running hard during this exercise, stop every once in a while and let him run out of line, or in other words, hit the end of the leash. When he comes close to you, pet him or verbally praise him. You want him to see the difference—being close to you will bring praise, and running away will bring the unyielding end of the leash.

If your dog is one of those tough guys with a neck of steel, move the choke collar up to the highest point on his neck just below his ears and place the ring of the collar at the bottom of his neck. This position puts the collar where he will be most sensitive to it. Another option would be to put a prong collar on him for the exercise.

This training session should take no more than *fifteen* minutes. If the session is done in the morning, you could repeat it for ten or fifteen minutes in the evening.

And, as with all training sessions, always end with a positive result.

Moses.

[CHAPTER 6]

The Heel Exercise

THE HEEL POSITION IS NOT SOMETHING YOU MAY be likely to use much, and it may be a challenge to learn, but once you understand it you will understand the fundamentals of training a dog. These fundamentals are: reading your dog, timing your corrections, and learning to effectively use leash angles—the angles made where your leash meets your dog's chain.

The Value of the Heel Exercise

Heel is a great exercise to use to teach your dog to pay attention to you. While your dog is "on a Heel" he must watch you to see what you want, or what direction you will take. Unlike the Break, where he can look around and sniff even though he's on a leash, on a Heel he can't smell the ground, look around, or stop whenever he wants. Heel also teaches *you* to read your dog. Watching your dog as you Heel gives you the opportunity to time a maneuver or make a correction that will keep his attention on you. By using your leash effectively when you make these corrections, you'll let the dog know that you expect him to look to you for direction. *You* are going to be the one who decides what you and your dog will be doing and when you'll be doing it. "Heel" makes this situation evident, and for this reason the Heel is a very important part in the foundation of dog obedience training.

You may encounter people who repeatedly call, "Heel, Heel, Heel," when they walk with their dog, because they feel that the dog should always be at their side when they go for a walk. This is not a correct use of Heel. Aside from training, the Heel is usually used for dog obedience competitions and isn't really a practical way to just "take a walk" with your dog. Later in the book you will learn a more practical, simplified way of walking with your dog at your side, called a "Patrol."

What "Heel" Means

When you give the command "Heel" to your dog, it means, "Get to my left side." From that position your dog will either sit at your side if you are standing still, or walk with you if you're walking. Heel is the second way to walk with your dog—walking on Break being the first—and it should be done with a loose leash. By that I mean that your leash should have enough slack so that you can make leash corrections that will be quick snaps, not pulls. Your dog should be shown what you want and given the chance to respond on his own, instead of being pulled along after you by a tight line.

Leash Position for Heel

For Heeling, place the loop of the leash around your right thumb and take up about two feet of slack. This is called your "reserve slack." As you see, about two feet of slack should be in your right hand, with about four feet of slack out between your hand and your dog's collar. Or put another way, about one-third of the leash should be held in your hand and two-thirds should be draped down. As your leash is draped down, it should always have a slight bend in it. It should fall in a loop just below your left knee before ending where it's attached to your dog's collar. This placement will ensure a loose leash so that you can make your corrections without pulling or steering your dog.

Correct leash position for beginning Heel.

Hold the leash with both your hands, and keep your hands together. As you Heel, you should work to *keep* your hands together. That way your corrections will tend to be stronger and better directed.

At a later time, when you don't have as much need for correction, you may be able to use only one hand—your right hand—to hold onto the leash for the Heel.

Right Turns

Before you can teach your dog to Heel you must first teach yourself how to turn. I know you believe you know how to turn, but I mean *really* turn, with sharp square angles. If you cannot make a square, *90-degree* turn, you will not be able to properly teach your dog to Heel. A square turn is *not* the same thing as a curved turn, or a turn in a circular manner. I have to work hard to get my clients to "square" their turns, not to "round" them.

Right-hand-only leash position for advanced Heel.

> *If you "round" your turn, you won't be able to give your dog the opportunity to make a square turn himself. And you won't have the opportunity to make a proper correction.*
> *If your turn is properly "squared," you'll give your dog the chance to make a clear change of direction with you.*

To begin learning to turn, we always start with a Right Turn, and we usually have clients try turning first without their dogs. You may also find it helpful to practice this on your own before you bring your dog into the lesson. To make this turn, pivot on your left foot and turn sharply at a right angle, taking the next step with your right foot. Be sure that you are pushing off, pivoting, with your left foot, not with both feet. Think of walking in a straight line, taking a step with the left foot forward, and then pivoting that on the ball of that foot so that you are then headed in a direction 90 degrees from the direction you were previously taking. To make that pivot, think of turning the ball of your foot as if you were putting out a cigarette or something else you wanted to extinguish.

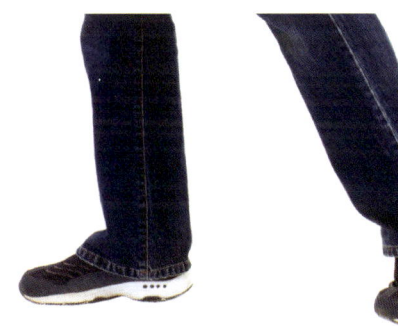

Always pivot with your left foot.

Using your feet to make square, sharp turns is an important part of the Heel exercise, but the way you handle your leash is equally important.

Let's say you've now pivoted with your left foot and have taken the next step with your right foot. As you make the *following step* with your left, look back at your dog and as you do, cock both hands holding the leash back to your left hip. Again, you should practice manipulating your leash and turning without having your dog with you, so that you have the chance to become comfortable with these maneuvers before you introduce them to him. Imagine that your hands are attached to your nose by a string, or a vertical line. When you look back, your hands, following the direction of your nose, will move back to your left hip.

By turning your head to look at your dog, you'll be able to see if he's going to make the turn with you or if he's going to keep heading in the direction you were both headed before the turn. By moving your hands back toward your left hip you'll be allowing your dog more leash and giving him the opportunity to turn with you instead of being pulled around. When you are comfortable making the turns and handling the leash on your own, put the leash on your dog, position yourself so that he is at your left side and give him the command, "Heel." As you step forward you should try to remember to step off with your *left foot first*. This will help your dog differentiate your commands, since you will be stepping off with your right foot first when you teach your dog the "Stay."

Cock your hands back and turn your head to see if your dog is coming.

After saying "Heel," take several steps forward, remembering to hold your hands together with your leash in the heel position, and then start making sharp right turns. If your dog is not paying attention to you and doesn't turn with you, he should get the same type of correction he would receive if he headed off in another direction while you were walking with him on Break. You guessed it—the "brick wall effect," or "quick snap and release."

When you make this correction, be sure that you *do not pull* your dog as is shown in the photo on the left! This photograph illustrates what happens if you do not bring your hands back to your hip after making the Right Turn. To correct your dog when you make the turn, you want to think of snapping your dog's collar, or chain. Pulling will not only be ineffective in correcting your dog, it will be hard on you—while jerking, or snapping, the collar properly will be effective in correcting your dog and much easier on you.

Do not pull your dog around the turn.

> *Remember this fact: it takes strength to pull the dog; it takes technique to snap the collar.*

If your dog *does* turn with you without the leash tightening, he should be verbally praised: "Good boy, good boy!" That's the way the turn game works. If he doesn't make the turn with you, he feels

the snap on the collar; if he does make the turn he hears the praise. You can use the Right Turn to keep his attention focused on you by taking a Right Turn just as he begins to walk ahead of you, or just as you see him take his eyes off you. In this way Heeling helps teach you to "read" your dog. By being aware and watching him as you Heel, you can see when his attention wanders and use Heeling maneuvers to bring his focus back to you. If you allow him to take his eye off you and look in another direction without receiving a correction, such as a sudden turn, your training will be inconsistent and you'll simply confuse your dog.

The Automatic Sit

When your dog is Heeling and you come to a stop, the dog must automatically Sit at your left side. By "automatically" I mean he must Sit without receiving a specific command from you or without you telling him to Sit.

Getting the Leash into Your Right Hand

Slide your left hand down the leash and lift the clip up.

Grasp the leash with your right hand.

To help you get your dog into the Automatic Sit the moment you come to a halt, it's useful to first practice getting the bulk of the leash into your right hand as soon as possible. Starting with your hands holding the leash in the Heel position—that would be both hands together—slide your left hand about halfway down the leash and pull in an upward motion to lift the clip up. In this manner you're using your left hand like a pulley, holding the lower part of the leash up so that you have a target for your right hand.

While you hold the loop of the leash with your ring finger and the little finger of your right hand, grasp the lower part of the leash using the rest of your right hand—your right index finger, middle finger, and thumb. *See the photo for clarification.*

When you've grabbed the lower part of the leash with your right fingers, completely release your hold on the leash with your left hand. You should find yourself holding the doubled up leash entirely with your right hand. Your left hand is then free to direct your dog's rear if necessary.

Your left hand can direct your dog's rear.

After your dog Sits, if you then release your grip on the leash with your right thumb, index finger, and middle finger, you should find yourself still holding the leash with your ring finger and little finger, and back in the Heel position where you began—holding your leash with about two feet of slack. You should practice this maneuver with your leash until you feel you can gather the entire leash into your right hand quickly. Practicing this maneuver with your leash attached to something else, like a kennel, is a good way to improve your technique before you try it with your dog. This maneuver is one of the most common control maneuvers you will need to know to handle your dog. It enables the trainer to always be ahead of the dog.

Standing Straight

When you're Heeling and you come to a halt, you must also be aware of the way you're standing. Stop as if your feet are planted in concrete, and stand as straight as possible. If you come to a halt with your body angled toward your dog, or if you stop and shift your position, he won't be sure where he's supposed to Sit.

If Your Dog Is Going to Pass You

If you come to a halt and it looks as though your dog is going to pass you, be ready to quickly slide your left hand about halfway back on the leash, angling toward his tail, to produce a quick tighten-and-release correction on the collar just after you make your stop. Try to make this correction at the exact time you are planting your last step. If you're fast enough you'll be able to stop your dog quickly and will start conditioning him to stop at the moment you stop. If you don't make your correction a quick tighten-and-release, and instead make it a tighten-and-pull, your dog will not be learning to stop with you on his own.

When you stop, stand straight.

If your dog is passing you, make a quick snap toward his tail.

Remember that there is a learning phase and a correction phase. After you've been placing your dog in the Sit position for a while, you must give him the opportunity to do it himself. If he doesn't Sit on his own when you come to a stop, make a correction. I usually give the dogs I train a few days of "showing" before "correcting."

If Your Dog Doesn't Sit Automatically

When you come to a stop and your dog doesn't Sit, quickly get the leash doubled up in your right hand (as previously described) and pull the leash up in front of your dog's nose at about a 45-degree angle. This should pull your dog's rear legs forward and force him into a Sit position. Since you're holding the leash entirely with your right hand at this point, your left is available to maneuver the dog's rear end into a straight position. Ideally you want your dog sitting straight at your left side, facing forward just as you are, but *patience is very important.* You want to move your dog into the Sit position by increments and give him verbal praise as he makes movements that approximate what you want.

Pull leash up at a 45-degree angle with your right hand.

If he refuses to Sit after a few pulls with the leash you can use your left hand to apply pressure to his rear. Remember: right hand at the front to control the front of the dog; left hand at the rear to direct the rear.

With your left hand press on his spine just above the hips at the same time you use your right hand to tighten the leash, pulling it upward in a 45-degree angle. Make sure you simultaneously tighten the leash and touch your dog's rear and then simultaneously release that pull and stop the pressure at his rear. **Do not push hard.** Just touch his rear end for a second. If you cannot get your dog to put himself into a Sit position by employing these techniques, tighten your leash and continue to pull it upward in that 45-degree angle until he Sits, then pet him.

If Your Dog Doesn't Sit Straight

You may come to a halt when Heeling and find that your dog doesn't Sit at your side facing ahead in a straightforward position. Instead his body may be twisted in such a way that he's angled away from you, with his rear positioned farther away from your side than his front legs are. If this happens you want to take appropriate

Move your left hand to adjust your dog's left side.

actions to get him to straighten out. Move your left hand around to his left side and press the area at his lowest rib, while at the same time you use your right hand to keep the leash held at a 45-degree angle in front of his face *(right hand at 45-degree angle, left hand on ribs, knees bent)*. As you do this be sure to keep your right hand a three-inch distance from the clip of the leash so that you have control of your dog's head.

Some dogs do not liked being touched at their sides, and when your left hand is reaching for your dog's rib, you do not want him to be able to turn and reach that hand with his mouth. If he does turn his head and attempt to reach for your left hand, use your right hand to give the leash a couple of quick snaps. Use this action to teach him that you are the one in charge. No biting or protesting from him will be allowed.

Your Position and Your Corrections

When you make corrections for the Sit, you want to start with as light a correction as possible and increase your pressure only as needed. Then as soon as you've made your correction, stand up straight. You want to start and end your corrections from a standing position. After you come to a halt, with your feet planted firmly, bend your knees to get the proper angles with the leash and to be able to use your left hand if necessary. Then return yourself immediately afterward to a standing position.

When You CAN Get Your Dog to Sit Automatically

As soon as your dog falls into the correct Sit position, give him hand praise. Stroke him with slow, calm strokes to encourage him and help him enjoy being in that position. After he Sits for a few seconds, and before he starts to get up, Break him by stepping backward as you give the command, "Break." Be sure to step backward, not forward, when you tell your dog to Break. You don't want him to confuse your movement with the forward direction you make when you want him to Heel.

The next step in teaching your dog to hold the Sit position longer will be to increase the time you require him to Sit before you Break him. You can start to increase the Sitting time to ten, twenty, then thirty seconds.

Go through the Heel exercise by telling him to Heel, making Right Turns, making him Sit when you halt, and then Breaking him. The Break you give him after making several turns will rejuvenate him and help ready him for the next set of turns you'll make. As your dog realizes that the Break is coming, he'll also be more eager to perform and to earn the next Break.

The Right–About Turn

The next turn you'll learn—the Right–About Turn—is very important. It gives you the opportunity to make a significant correction if your dog is not following you properly.

Pivot and move your hands back to your left hip.

Check to see your dog's progress.

You'll make this turn just as you would a Right Turn—by pivoting on your left foot. The difference will be that instead of making a *90*-degree turn after you pivot, you'll make a *180*-degree turn. In other words, instead of turning to your right, you'll turn directly backward and head in the completely opposite direction. And just as you checked to see if your dog was following when you made a Right Turn, you must check his progress when you make a Right–About. After you turn, cock both hands back to your left hip just as you did before.

This maneuver will be easier if you remember to hold your leash *low* with your hands *together* as you Heel. Also remember to imagine your hands being connected to your nose—as your head turns back, your hands will also move back toward your left hip. When you look back to see if he's going to turn with you, be sure you give him the chance to make the turn before giving a correction.

If he's moving fast ahead of you, as you make the Right–About Turn drop the two feet of your reserve slack. You can then brace yourself like a brick wall, and as he hits the end of that reserve slack he'll receive a significant correction.

On a Heel your dog should never allow you the opportunity to release your reserve slack. He should be walking on your left with his head even with your upper body and making turns as you make turns.

Practice Heeling with Right Turns and the Automatic Sit for about ten minutes twice a day. It's worth your effort.

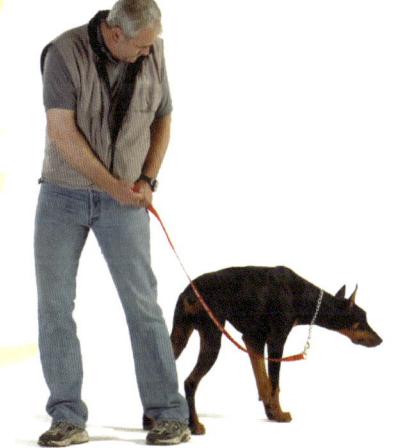
Drop your slack if he isn't making the Right-About Turn with you.

Remember that by learning the Heeling exercise you'll be learning: to make the angle of the leash *work for you, to* time your corrections *so that they are most effective, and to* read your dog *so you'll know when to act (make a correction) to bring his focus back to you.*

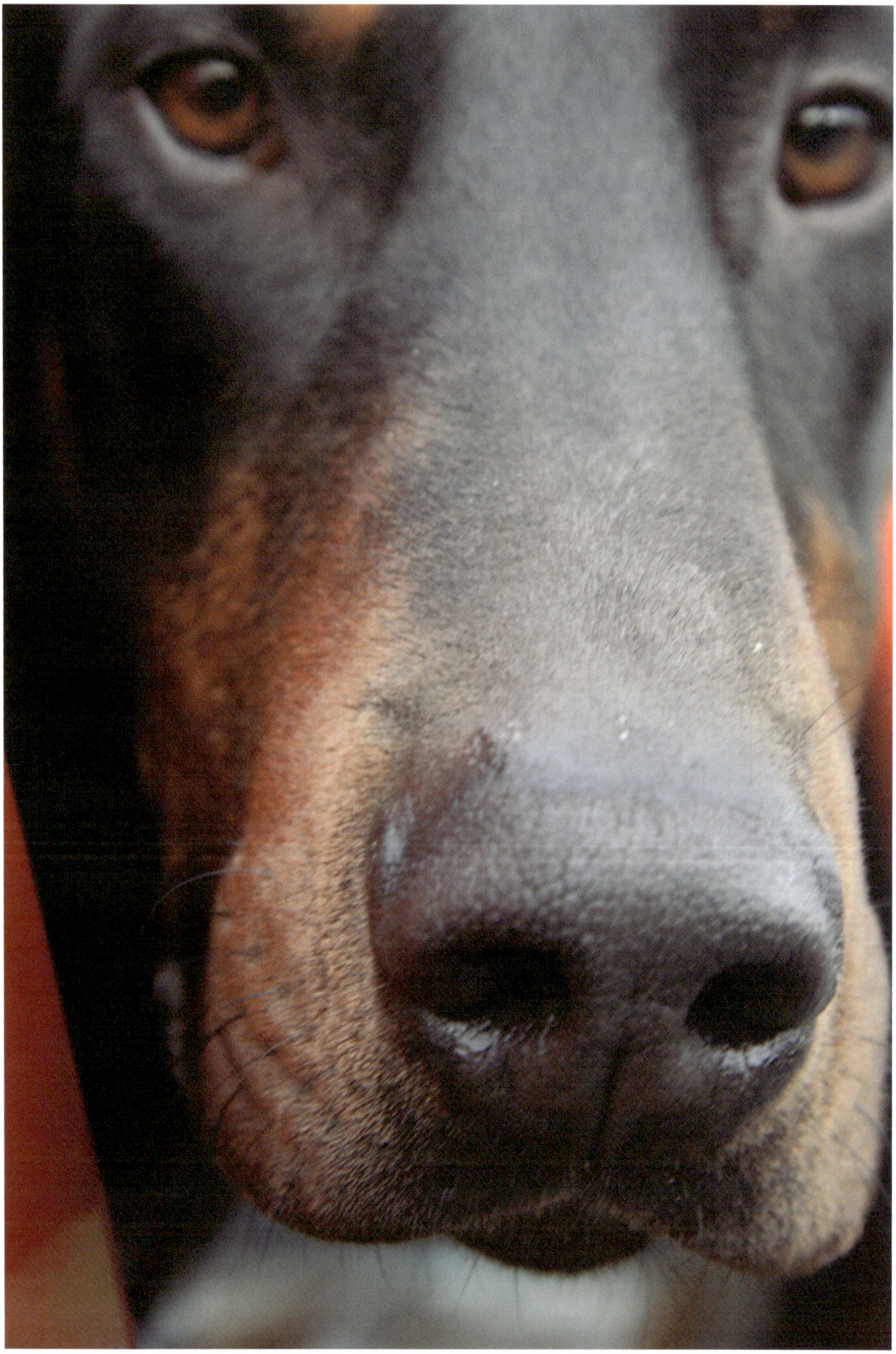

Moses.

[CHAPTER 7]

More Heeling Maneuvers

NOW THAT YOU'RE ACQUAINTED WITH RIGHT TURNS, Right–Abouts, and the Automatic Sit, you're ready to add the rest of the Heeling maneuvers. By mastering them you can really make Heeling a useful exercise to keep your dog's attention on you.

The Side Step

There are three different side steps. Each is designed to help you keep your dog Heeling close to your left side and to teach him to keep his eye on you.

Side Step to the Side

When your dog is wandering farther to the left than you want, you can make a side step to your right. While you continue moving forward, step sideways

Sidestep to the right to bring your dog in closer.

with your right foot and then bring your left foot over to meet your right without stopping your forward motion.

As you bring your left foot over, give a quick snap to the right with your leash so that your dog will feel a sharp snap on his collar. Only make this snap with your leash if your dog is not making the rightward move with you in time.

If he is making the move and staying close by your left side, give him verbal praise instead.

As you make the side step, be sure you continue walking forward in a straight-ahead direction instead of *veering off to the right*.

Give a quick snap to the right with your leash.

Continue walking forward as you sidestep.

Side Step Back

This maneuver can be used when your dog is moving ahead of you and to the left. It can be used in place of a Right–About to correct his too-far-forward behavior and has the advantage of letting you stay headed in the direction you've chosen. Again you'll take a side-ways step with your right foot, but this time you'll take the step to the right and backward, moving your left foot back and giving your leash a sharp snap back and to the right at the same time.

Sidestep back if your dog moves too far ahead.

Sidestep ahead if your dog lags behind.

Side Step Forward

Sometimes your dog may lag behind and to the left. In this case you can take a side step ahead, moving your right foot *forward* and to the right, and making a sharp snap forward and to the right as you move your left foot toward your right.

Left Turn

You should be able to turn freely to your left without having your dog interfere with your turn by forging too far ahead of you. To make a Left Turn, pivot on the ball of your left foot and turn your body 90 degrees to the left. As you make the turn, raise your right knee up in a march-like step. Your right knee should just brush past the front of your left knee. When you make this maneuver the change of direction will be clear to your dog, and if his head is moving too far forward he'll get bumped with your right knee.

Your dog's head should not be too far in front of your left leg.

Raise your right knee as you make the Left Turn.

If you can move your right knee up fast enough he'll be startled by it and will begin to watch out for it. He'll come to realize that being ahead of you when Heeling is not the place he wants to be.

If your dog is very small you may want to alter this maneuver a bit, since a sharp upward-moving right knee may miss him entirely. Instead of raising your right knee up in a march-like step, you may find it more effective to swing your right foot over so that your dog receives a bump from your right shin if he's Heeling too far forward.

Left–About

Raise your right knee and continue with a march-like step.

Once you're making clean Left Turns without correction, you're ready to start Left–Abouts. A Left–About is made the same way the Left Turn is made. You just extend the turn to go all the way around 180 degrees to your left. This means that after you've turned you'll be headed in exactly the opposite direction. As you turn, keep a march-like step when you raise your right knee, and then follow with a march-like step of your left. If your dog is Heeling too close to you or trying to forge ahead of you he'll get bumped by your knees and cut off before he can move ahead. In this way you'll be teaching him to look out for you—the leader.

Changing Your Pace

If your dog is lagging behind you can speed up with one fast step, as if you were stepping over a mud puddle. This sudden step forward should cause a quick tightening and release of your dog's collar. You can then slow down to your normal pace and watch for him to lag again. In making this maneu-

Change your pace if your dog lags behind.

ver you must be careful that you don't pull your dog forward. His collar must tighten and release for only a fraction of a second. You can repeat this change of pace—speeding-up, then changing to a normal or slow walk—until you have your dog walking next to you with his head lined up with your body. At that point you can add verbal praise.

Using Heeling Maneuvers to Correct

Remember that the purpose of Heeling is to provide a vehicle for you to "read" your dog and teach him to keep his attention on you. You want to be able to figure out what his next move will be so that you can counter it with a move in the opposite direction—thereby forcing him to keep his eyes on you. As he learns to respond to your turns he will get faster at taking his eyes on and off you. Each Heeling maneuver is designed to help you keep your dog in the correct Heeling position, and in doing so, to help you gain focused attention from your dog.

To Review:

IF YOUR DOG IS BOLTING AHEAD OF YOU: You can counter his movement by making a right-about turn (and releasing your slack) to let him experience the "brick-wall effect" if he is continuing to head forward.

IF YOUR DOG IS MOVING A LITTLE BIT AHEAD OF YOU: Make a sharp Left Turn, bumping his head with your right knee as your right leg rises up in a sudden march-like step. You can also make a side step back, with a sharp jerk backward and to the right with your leash.

IF YOUR DOG IS LAGGING BEHIND: Change pace and speed up, then slow down. Make him watch to see what you're going to do next.

IF YOUR DOG IS HEELING TOO FAR TO THE LEFT: Make a side step, giving your leash a sharp snap to the right as your left foot moves toward your right. Or make a Right Turn.

> *To make the corrective action of all these maneuvers as effective as possible, be sure to work on your timing.*

MORE HEELING MANEUVERS • 67

Riley.

[CHAPTER 8]

"Stay"

TEACHING YOUR DOG THIS COMMAND NOT ONLY GIVES you the chance to encourage his concentration on you, it also helps you see that with training you're teaching your dog to understand what your commands mean. In essence: you must know what you mean when you give a command, before you can expect your dog to know what you mean.

What "Stay" Means

Before you teach your dog any new command you must first know precisely what that command means. If you give the same command when you want different behaviors, how can you expect your dog to know which behavior you want?

For example, often when I ask dog owners what they tell their dogs when they exit the car and want the dog to remain in the vehicle, nine out of ten will say, "Stay." Then I'll ask, "What command do you give your dog when you want him to stay in a Sit position in one place on your kitchen floor?" Their answer will usually be, "Stay."

Now my question is this: "If your dog can move around in your car as long as he doesn't get out on a Stay command, why would it not be all right if he walked around your kitchen on the same command?"

"Stay" to your dog should mean "Don't change your position."

> *Do not give one command and mean two (or more) different things. One command should expect one behavior.*

Start from the Heel position.

Give the "Stay" command and hand signal.

Be ready to stop your dog if he starts to move.

Leaving Your Dog on a Stay

To teach your dog the Stay command, start the lesson with your dog sitting in the Heel position at your left side, and yourself holding the leash with your hands in the Heel position. Next remove your left hand from the leash and place it in front of the dog with your palm facing his muzzle. As you move your palm in front of him give the command, "Stay."

Be sure to put your left hand back on the leash before you make the next move, which is to take a step forward. With your left hand there you'll be ready in case you need to slide it down the leash and jerk upward to stop your dog if he starts to move when you take that forward step.

Now move by stepping forward with your *right* foot as you pivot with your left, turning so that you face your dog and block him with your body. This helps him understand you want him to stay where he is and not go with you. At this point you should be a few inches in front of him. Remember, if he moves at any time up to this point you can slide your left hand down the leash and jerk it up in the air to stop him and keep him in his original position.

Once you feel he's settled, drop the slack of your leash and "switch thumbs," placing your left thumb in the leash loop where your right thumb was. (If you're left-handed, you do not need to switch thumbs at this point.)

Then back up slowly. As you back up, be conscious of the slack of the leash. You do not want the leash to tighten so that you inadvertently "pull" your dog out of his Sitting position. As you back up you should also be ready to slide your right hand halfway down the leash toward the clip so that you can snap upward to stop your dog and put him back into a Sitting position if he begins to rise. Be especially aware of his movements as you step backward, since this is a time when he is most likely to break his Sitting/Staying position.

Drop the slack of your leash and switch thumbs.

Back up slowly.

Step forward and put your dog back into a Sit if he moves.

Take him back with small tugs.

If he should get up on all fours before you can stop him, take him back to his original position by making small tugs—tightening and releasing his collar, trying to get him to walk with you—as you direct him back.

Then turn him so that he's again facing you and pull your leash upward in a 45-degree angle to bring him into a Sit. Once you have him Sitting, drop your slack and repeat your attempt to back up slowly while he remains in that position.

Pull your leash upward to bring him back into a Sit.

Returning to Your Dog

After you've managed to back up while your dog holds the Stay position, wait about five seconds and then return to him before he moves. To return to your dog, first switch thumbs again.

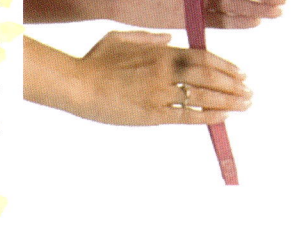

Now your right thumb will be back in the leash loop and your left hand will be the hand that's ready to slide down the leash and correct your dog if he starts to break his position.

To return, first switch thumbs.

When you've made this switch, slowly veer to your right, preparing to circle behind your dog and return to the Heel position where you stood when you first began the exercise. As you approach him and start to move behind him, hold the leash above your dog's head with your left hand about six inches from the clip. Do not tighten the leash, just be ready to snap it upward with your left hand if he should begin to break his Sit. You should also be ready to reach over his back with your right hand to stop his hind end from swinging out away from you if he starts to get up.

Have your left hand ready to slide down the leash.

As you move around your dog, hold the leash above his head.

When you are behind him, watch him closely for signs of moving.

Watch him closely. As you move behind him, out of his line of vision, he may be inclined to move himself. If he moves out of the Sit at any time as you circle around him, try to stop him before he manages to completely stand up. Your timing is very important. It will go a long way toward making your corrections as effective as possible and help you succeed in teaching your dog not to move when you say Stay.

If your dog lacks the confidence to sit still while you walk behind him, slide your left hand down the leash and rub his left ear to help keep him content as you move around him. Try using this rubbing maneuver a few times until he's more comfortable with you circling him.

If you need to comfort him, rub his ear as you circle.

A successful "return to your dog" should end with him sitting in the Heel position and you standing next to him, both of you in the same place you were before you said Stay.

To end this exercise tell your dog "Break," and step backward, making it clear to him that he's "at ease."

A successful return should have you back in the Heel position.

Introducing Distractions

As your workouts continue, build up the amount of time your dog must hold the Stay. For the first day a five- to ten-second Stay is fine, but after a few sessions he should be able to hold at least a one-minute Stay. Then introduce some distractions, such as a person walking by or a ball rolling past. At the end of the first "Stay session" at our facility I try calling a client's dog and have the client make a correction if the dog responds to my command. I want my clients to teach their dogs to be concerned only with their masters' commands, no one else's. If you want to try this yourself, just be sure you do not have a family member do the calling, because that is a person you want your dog to go to.

Coco.

[CHAPTER 9]

"Come"

WHEN YOUR DOG HAS LEARNED THE STAY, YOU'RE READY to start teaching him to follow your commands even when he's separated from you by the distance of your six-foot leash.

On-leash Come

To teach your dog what "Come" means, start by leaving him on a Stay and backing up as far as the end of your leash—just as you backed up in the previous lesson when you taught him the Stay. At this point you should be standing with your left thumb in the leash loop and your right hand ready to slide down the leash and stop him if he moves.

Signal with your right hand as you say, "Come."

Next let go of your leash with your right hand, and use your right hand and arm to make a sweeping arc toward yourself while you say, "Come." As you give your command and hand signal, back up a few steps to help draw your dog toward you. If he doesn't move, make a slight snap with your leash, and remember that you want to snap the *collar,* not the *dog.* If he still doesn't move toward you, repeat the snap and take another step backward at the same time.

As your dog approaches you give him verbal praise—"Gooood boy"—and *gather the slack* of your leash. The most effective way to gather the slack is to bring the leash through the fingers of your right hand as though you were pulling thread through a needle. You want to have the leash gathered in your hands and not lying on the ground by the time the dog reaches you.

Gather the slack of your leash as your dog approaches.

If your dog is fast and comes at you before you have the chance to gather the slack of your leash, back up more before you stop. Give yourself the chance to bring in the leash before he arrives. You want to be in control so that you can handle your leash effectively.

As your dog approaches, you should also watch the direction he's taking. You want to bring him *straight to you* so that he ends up directly in front of you. If he heads off to one side of you, you can correct him by making a quick snap on his collar to head him back toward you.

Also watch for him to come toward you and then attempt to pass you. If he tries to do this, catch him with a quick snap on his collar just as he starts to pass.

The Sit-in-Front

When the dog is standing in front of you and you have the slack of the leash gathered, move your leash clip around so that it is under your dog's neck. To get your clip to this position you may have to slide the chain around your dog's neck in a counterclockwise direction so that the ring of the choke chain is underneath your dog's mouth. With your leash clip in this position you're ready to pull your dog into a Sit by pulling the leash upward and toward you. The angle of the pull should begin at about a 45-degree angle and continue upward.

When you have your dog Sitting in front of you for the first time, stand up straight, give him verbal praise, and then Break him.

Pull your dog into a Sit using a 45-degree leash angle.

At first your goal in teaching your dog to Come on-leash should be to get the dog to Sit in front of you when you call him. Initially you don't want to be concerned if he's sitting at a crooked angle, instead of being directly straight before you. But as you practice this exercise and he becomes aware of what you want him to do—come to you and Sit in front when he's called—you can improve his Sit-in-front position by straightening him out this way:

Improve the "Sit in front" by straightening your dog's position.

Direct the angle of the Sit by first lifting the dog's rear.

If he's leaning to your left, press just below his right ribs with your left hand. If he's leaning to your right, press just below his left ribs with your right hand. Make sure when you touch the dog's rib area you also tighten up your leash in that 45-degree angle. I never try to shift a dog's rear area by hand without simultaneously controlling his front area by leash.

By tightening (pulling) the leash at a 45-degree angle toward your own hip, you are lifting the dog's rear at the same time you're directing the angle of his Sit by pressing below the rib area. The dog's rear must be lifted before you can redirect it to the spot where you want him to Sit.

How To Practice

You can practice Come on-leash by repeatedly leaving your dog on a Stay, backing up, and calling him using your Come command and hand signal. Be aware that you do not need to return to the Heel position each time you want to tell your dog to Stay. You can tell him to Stay as he Sits in front of you by putting your right hand in front of his face and saying "Stay" before you back up.

> *Remember that each time you back away, or "leave your dog," you must tell him "Stay" if you expect him to remain in that position until he is released from it.*

When you're practicing you can vary your movements by sometimes calling him to you for the Sit-in-front, and

Tell your dog "Stay" before you leave him.

Give your dog calm hand and verbal praise.

sometimes leaving him, backing up, and returning to him—placing yourself back in the Heel position.

When your dog Comes at your command and Sits in front of you, give him some calm hand and verbal praise while you stand up straight. You want to teach him that just because you're petting him doesn't mean he's released.

He can't get up and move around unless you give him permission to do so. Pet him with your free hand and be ready to stop him with your leash hand. As you practice you want to gradually build the time your dog can Sit in front of you, be praised, and still hold the Sit.

When the Sit-in-Front Is Not Required

When you call your dog he is only required to Sit directly in front of you if you are standing straight and waiting for his approach. If you call him and then bend down to pet him, or change your position to greet him, or turn away before he reaches you, he is not required to Sit in front of you.

By altering your position you interrupt, or alter, his target; and in that case he only needs to come to you, not sit before you. For instance, if you call your dog with "Come" as you walk away, he only needs to join you and go along with you in order to have answered your command correctly.

Squints.

[CHAPTER 10]

The Finish

UP TO THIS POINT, WHEN YOU TOLD YOUR DOG "Heel," you moved forward or positioned yourself with your dog at your left to make the Heel exercise easier for him to learn. With the Finish, your dog will bring himself to the Heel position on his own.

What "Finishing" Your Dog Means

Finishing your dog means that when you tell and/or signal your dog to Heel he will come to your left side and either sit or walk with you on a Heel. If you are standing still he must come to the left side (Heel position) and sit. If you are walking he must come to the left side (Heel position) and walk with you. If he is in front of you when you tell him to Heel, he should walk toward you, come around your right side, circle behind you, and sit at your left side. If he's already left of you or behind you when you say "Heel," he doesn't have to circle you, he can just move to your left side.

To teach your dog how to get to his owner's left, no matter what his position may be when he hears the command "Heel," you will start by having him come around behind you and then move to your left.

Finish from Break

To teach your dog the Finish while he's on a Break, first position yourself so that he is ahead of you and take the leash in your left hand. As you say "Heel," signal your command by making a passing motion with your right hand.

Signal "Heel" with your right hand.

When you make this motion your right arm should be straight at your right hip as your hand gestures back toward your rear. As soon as you've signaled, transfer your leash from your left hand to your right and take about three steps backward.

If your dog is not moving in the direction you signaled (to your right), give his collar a quick snap to get him to move that way. By moving backward and making that snap you're drawing the dog toward you, then behind you, all from your right side.

As he comes around behind you, bring your right hand behind your back and transfer the leash to your left hand. Now take three steps forward *without pulling the dog around you,* and as you move forward look back to see if he's following you. If he's not following, give a quick snap to his collar to get him to walk in the direction your leash should be aiming—forward.

Throughout this maneuver you want to be sure to keep your leash ahead of your dog. You want to use your leash to show him the direction he's to follow, but you want to be sure that you aren't putting tension on it.

If your leash is tight you'll more likely be pulling your dog around you instead of showing him the direction he's to take. You want him to do this—circle around you and follow you forward—on his own, and not because he's being pulled in these directions. Constant pressure on his leash could also cause him to stop and tense up.

Keep your eye on your dog and check his progress as you back up and then come forward. If he's following your direction well you may not need to make any corrections—quick snaps—with the leash. Instead you can give him verbal praise to encourage him and let him know that he's doing what you want.

Transfer the leash to your right hand.

Switch the leash to your left as you draw the dog behind you.

Keep your leash ahead of your dog.

At this point in learning the Finish you want to take enough steps backward and then forward to draw the dog with you and have him follow the direction you're taking. If you stop—either as you move backward or before you reverse direction and start to go forward—your dog will stop or slow down. If that occurs you're likely to begin pulling him.

After he has come with you as you took the three steps forward, halt and put him into a Sit at your side. Do not give him the Sit command. As with the Heel, the Automatic Sit is part of the Finish.

Later on, after your dog is familiar with the Finish, you should be able to reduce the number of steps you're taking backward and forward. Eventually you should reach the point where you can tell the dog "Heel," and he will come toward you, circle you, and sit at your left side while you remain standing still. Once he gets the hang of it, if he stops at any point you can then back up and give a correction, thereby teaching him not to stop.

Put your dog into a Sit by your side.

Finish from the Sit-in-Front Position

You can also Finish your dog when he's Sitting directly in front of you after you called him to come. In this case make the same hand signal—a quick motion backward with your right hand—as you say "Heel."

After that just follow through as you did with the Finish from Break. Transfer the leash from your left hand to your right, take three steps backward, switch the leash from your right hand to your left behind your back, take three steps forward, halt, and get him to Sit. Again remember to check behind you as you start to come forward, to see that your dog is moving forward with you. And be sure to give him verbal praise as he follows what you want him to do.

Signal with "Heel" from the "Sit in front" position.

When you give the Heel command and he gets up and starts heading back around you on his own without a snap of the leash, you can start reducing the number of steps you're taking backward and forward. Move to taking one step back and one step forward and eventually to standing still while your dog comes around you to Sit at your left.

"Finish" ends with your dog in the Heel position.

Three Important Things to Remember as You Practice the Finish

- Use your leash to give your dog direction. (Don't use it to *pull* your dog around you.)
- Don't stop or slow down as you move backward and then forward. (If you stop your dog will stop.)
- The moment your dog takes any steps in the right direction *be sure to verbally praise him.*

THE FINISH • 87

Jayda.

[CHAPTER 11]

Down and Sit from the Side

DOWN IS A SUBMISSIVE POSITION, AND MOST DOMINANT dogs are not eager to be submissive. Since your dog may be one of those, or one that just does not want to submit to you and follow this command, accomplishing this lesson might be a challenge. But if done properly, teaching your dog the Down will be a very important breaking point for you in achieving dominance over your dog—and a big step forward in receiving true obedience from him.

What "Down" Should Mean to Your Dog

Using one command to mean one behavior is as important with Down as it is with Stay. When you tell your dog "Down," it should mean "Hit the ground and do not move until I give you another command." It should *not* mean "Get off me," or "Get off the furniture," or "Get off the counter." If you want to give a command that means "get off something" use "Off."

There is a big difference between your dog's lying down when he's bored, or when you coax him with a treat, as opposed to him dropping down anytime, anywhere, because you told him "Down." Even if you tell your dog "Down" and he doesn't go Down at once, it's very important that when you start to correct him he gives in and drops to the ground without resistance.

Value of "Down"

Not only is your dog's compliance with this command a valuable means of establishing your control over him, it also provides some very useful functions. I used it once when I was walking down a logging road and saw a car coming. My dog was at the side of the road and I commanded him with "Down." He then dropped and remained in that position until the car passed and I gave him the Break command.

I've also used the Down in emergency situations. I remember a time when I was at a beach and two dogs suddenly came running toward my dog and me. I immediately Downed my dog so he wouldn't appear to be a challenge to the other dogs. When your dog is lying down he is in a passive position because of the body posture. He cannot very well stand tall, raise his tail, and be dominant when he's lying down, so in the eyes of another dog that means he's less of a threat. In this case I also stepped in front of him so that I could protect him, and he wouldn't have to protect himself.

Teaching the Down to Your Dog

Because this lesson is challenging, it's important to give yourself every advantage for success.

To begin with, it's helpful to start your lesson on a carpeted area. This surface will make it easier for your dog to get into the Down position and to rise from it. Aside from the carpeting advantage, indoors can be an excellent place to start teaching the Down as there may be fewer distractions there than there are outdoors. In any case you want to make sure that distractions are minimized. For example, have your dog facing a doorway instead of having his back to it. You don't want him to be concerned that something is going on behind him that will compete for his attention.

In teaching the Down I follow a series of three techniques. If the first isn't effective, I move to the second, and if that one is not effective, I move to the third. The series is as follows:

1. A light touch on the leash with your left foot.
2. Using your left foot on the leash together with your left hand on your dog's back (behind his shoulder blades).
3. Crouching down and using your right hand to pull your leash downward while pressing on your dog's back with your left hand.

Extend your arm to give the "Down" command.

THE FIRST TECHNIQUE: To teach your dog the Down, you want to begin with him sitting at your left side on a carpeted surface. To get there you could Heel with him, come to a halt, and get him into the Automatic Sit. At this point you should be holding the leash with your hands in the Heel position.

From this position, you should have enough slack in your leash to have a target for your left foot to hit. Next give the command "Down" as you extend your left arm straight out, parallel to the ground. As soon as you've given your command and hand/arm signal, *lower your left arm. Do not leave your arm extended.*

Start to raise your left leg slowly and press on the leash lightly with your left foot to show your dog the direction you want him to take.

Be sure you don't press your leash all the way to the ground. You want your dog to feel a light downward pressure from your foot on the leash, and he won't feel this if the leash is lying flat against the ground.

Start to raise your left leg to press on your leash.

Press downward gently with your foot.

Give another downward press with your foot.

Immediately after pressing on the leash, *put your left foot back on the ground*, regain your balance, and *wait*, giving your dog the chance to go down. In the beginning, do not push too hard with your foot, or your dog will resist and you'll end up in a battle.

Using your left foot for showing direction in this manner may seem awkward in the beginning, but later, when your dog understands what this pressure on the leash means, it will be an easy and convenient way to correct him.

If, after doing the press with your foot, you see that your dog is not showing any sign of movement in a downward direction, put your left foot back on the leash and give it another light push. Again, remove your foot immediately, regain your balance, and give him the chance to go down.

Watch your dog carefully to determine whether he's expressing any desire to bend his front legs and attempt to go down.

It's likely that in the beginning your dog will try to get up out of his Sit position instead of lie down. In this case you want to stop him as quickly as you can by sliding your left hand down the leash and giving a tug toward your dog's tail. If this move fails to stop him from getting up, you'll need to move him back into the Sit position before you can try again. To place him into the Sit, move your right hand to a place on the leash about four inches from the clip and pull upward at a 45-degree angle from his nose, just as you did when you were teaching him the Automatic Sit in the Heel exercise. At the same time you pull you should have your left hand available to direct his rear end if it's necessary. Once your dog is back in the Sit position, immediately repeat the "press" procedure with your left foot. Press on the leash, then put your foot back on the ground. If, after your third or fourth attempt, your dog will still not go down, proceed to the second technique.

THE SECOND TECHNIQUE: When you press on the leash with your left foot, place your left hand behind your dog's shoulder blades while your right hand holds the leash. There is a pressure point just behind your dog's shoulder blades that you should aim for. With your left hand open, the pressure on his back should come mainly from your left thumb. However, if your dog is leaning to one side or the other, try to apply pressure with either your thumb or finger in the same direction your dog is leaning. In other words, encourage your dog's downward movement by encouraging him to move in the direction of least resistance.

In this manner you can try to place him in the down by using your left foot to press on the leash while at the same time applying pressure to his back with your left hand. Remember: you do not want to press your left foot all the way to the ground. Employing this technique will be a bit of a balancing act for you, but it will pay off if you can do it. If, after your third or fourth attempt, your dog will still not go down, move to the third technique.

THE THIRD TECHNIQUE: Place your right hand on the leash about four inches from the clip—just as you did when you were putting him back into the Sit—and use that hand to control his front end. At the same time move your left hand to a place on his back just *rear* of his shoulder blades.

Remember to aim for that pressure point just behind your dog's shoulder blades. If you apply a small amount of pressure there with your left thumb as you pull the leash in a down and forward direction with your right hand, your dog will go down. Keep the knuckles of your right hand facing toward the ground as you pull forward with your leash.

It's best not to use a large amount of force when you employ this technique—especially if you feel your dog brace up to resist you. As you use your leash at his front and apply pressure to his back,

try to tip him sideways. If he seems to be leaning in one direction or another, press with more force in that direction. You should try this several times in a gentle manner.

Always use the downward tug with your leash and the pressure from your left hand simultaneously. *And be sure to pause, or let go, between tugs to give your dog the chance to go down before you make another tug on his leash!*

If your dog is a tough guy and persists in bracing himself instead of giving in, another option you might try is the use of a prong collar. You would be following the same procedure you followed before, just with the added pressure of this type of collar.

Place your left hand to the rear of his shoulder blades.

Tug the leash in a downward and forward direction.

To summarize this lesson, when you teach your dog "Down" from the Heel position, always start showing him what you want by raising your left foot and making a press or two with your left foot on the leash. If he still won't go Down despite the pressure from your foot, you can then add the technique of pressing on the leash with your left foot while pressing on his back (behind his shoulder blades) with your left hand. If he still won't go down with the use of those two techniques, bring your right hand down on the leash and tug the leash downward while you press with your left hand on your dog's back behind his shoulder blades.

When your dog does go Down, by whichever technique, squat next to him, and keep your right hand on the leash just above the clip as you stroke him calmly from neck to rear with your left hand.

At this point you only want him staying Down for about five seconds, and you want to be sure to Break him before he gets up. This will show him that when he goes Down you will pet him and give him a Break. Once he's experienced the positive feeling associated with your hand

Stroke your dog calmly when he goes down.

praise and the fast Break he'll be much more willing to go Down the next time you tell him. Never hold him down—that will make him want to resist you.

Once you get your dog to go Down a few times and he relaxes and enjoys the hand praise, try to stand up straight and give him some slow verbal praise before you Break him.

Before I end a first session of this lesson I expect a dog to go Down at least once or twice as soon as I tap the leash with my left foot. This could take more than half an hour, especially if he is doing a lot of resisting. If you find yourself feeling frustrated, hang it up for the day and try later. Again, this not an easy lesson to accomplish without having me standing there guiding you through it step-by-step, so if you get impatient, quit and try again the next day.

Practicing the Down

As mentioned before, it may help to work on this lesson while your dog is in the house and can lie on the carpet. After he's mastered the Down indoors you can work your way up to wet grass or harder, less comfortable surfaces.

If you practice the Down two or three times a day for short sessions, he will start to go Down just as you raise your left foot. Make the workout very short if you see that your dog is performing better than he did in the previous workout.

Your dog should go down at just the raise of your foot, then at your command only.

After two or three workouts when your dog is going Down at the raise of your left foot, you should start to expect him to go Down on your command—that is, he should drop when you say "Down," instead of when he sees the threat of a correction (your left foot positioning to press on the leash.)

To help him get to this point you can make your corrections faster. As you stand next to him in the Heel position, let out more slack from the reserve of leash line you are holding in your right hand. Have the loop of the leash hanging about three to four inches from the ground next to your left foot. Give your dog the Down command then immediately—within a half-second—give the leash a quick downward snap with your left foot. You can repeat this procedure until you see your dog try to "beat you to the draw" and drop before you can tap on the leash. When he does this be sure to give him verbal praise and a Break.

Problems You May Encounter

When you are teaching your dog the Down you may find that he will *roll over on his side or back* instead of lying straight beside you. To correct this problem, first let him have the chance to get comfortable on his back or side—this can take only a moment—then give the Heel command and instantly start walking forward, left foot first, without giving him the chance to roll back over. As you start forward, give him a good hard pull with your leash and then release the tension so that he has the chance to get up and walk with you.

In this case it's important that you pull him about a foot or so while he's lying on his back or side instead of allowing him to get up on his own. If executed properly, this maneuver should cause him to scramble to get up and go with you, and it shouldn't be an experience he'd want to repeat indefinitely.

After moving forward with your dog, halt and give him the Down command. If he lies on his side or back again, repeat the procedure of telling him to Heel, moving forward, and pulling him from his position. After he lies straight at your side on a Down command, move forward on a Heel as you praise him verbally. When that happens he'll be praised for lying straight and will see that from that position he has time to get up and go with you when you start to move forward.

Your dog may roll on his side instead of lying straight.

Another problem may be that you see your dog start *to inch forward* on his belly when he's in the Down position. If this happens, immediately slide your left hand down the leash and toward the rear of your dog while making a quick snap, then stand up instantly without letting him see you make the correction. If he sees you he'll most likely get up. In that event you'd better be ready to catch him with your left foot correction.

If your dog gets up from the Down before you have either given him a Break command or moved forward on a Heel, place him back into a Sit and immediately press on your leash with your left foot. You want to place him back in the Down position just the way you did when you were teaching it to him. Do not repeat your "Down" command. Just correct your dog by showing him that he still needs to be lying down.

Correct your dog for inching forward.

Correct for sniffing the ground without causing your dog to rise.

If your dog is sniffing the ground while in the Down position, you need to stop this behavior or he will start creeping forward. Your natural tendacy may be to jerk your leash upward, but that action would bring your dog up into the Sit position. Instead, the moment he goes to sniff, you must quickly put your foot at the side of his neck on the choke collar and then immediately release your foot. The correction should only last about one second. You must not hold him down. This action will stop your dog's sniffing and still keep him down. If he does get up, patiently work him back into a Down again.

Sit from the Down Position

When your dog is dropping down pretty consistently when you say "Down," you can add the Sit command. While your dog is lying beside you, transfer your leash over to your left hand and pick up any slack so that your left arm is straight at your side while you're holding your leash. Use your right hand to make a sweeping arc, as if you were scooping up air with open palm, right before your dog's face. As you make this hand signal, give your dog the command "Sit." Just after you give your command, give his collar a light snap with the leash in your left hand, and watch to see if he will make an effort to get up using only his front legs.

Transfer the leash to your left hand.

Make a sweeping arc with your right hand.

Give the "Sit" command as you signal.

If he doesn't try to get up, repeat the snap on his collar, and then start to lift him with your leash until he is in the Sit position. Lift him part way, part way, into the Sit. You want to let him take steps

Lift your dog by increments into the Sit.

to get into the Sit position, just as he took steps to get into the Down position. Once he is in the Sit, stroke him.

When your dog shows any signs of getting into the Sit position on his own without your corrections, be sure to verbally praise him. Let him have time to get into the Sit. If he gets there all the way on his own, give him hand and verbal praise and then Break him. That Break command will be the ultimate reward for him.

Jayda.

[CHAPTER 12]

Down and Sit from the Front

ONCE YOUR DOG IS RESPONDING TO "DOWN FROM THE SIDE" you can move to telling your dog to Down when you are not standing directly next to him. This will increase your control over your dog and make it possible for you to use the "Down" command in many other situations.

"Down" from the Front

To teach your dog to Down when you are standing in front him, leave him on a Stay and back up to the end of your leash. You can get there by Finishing your dog, telling him "Stay," and backing up just as you did when you worked on the lesson of Come on-leash. You want to back up the length of your leash but still allow enough slack so that the leash loop lies about six to eight inches from the ground.

At this point you should have the leash loop in your left thumb (assuming you're right-handed) and be ready to make a clear signal with your right hand. (If you're left-handed the hand designations are just the opposite.) To signal, put your right hand and arm straight out in front of you, parallel to the ground, as you say "Down,"

Signal the Down with your right arm straight in front of you.

Step forward with your left foot.

Press on the leash with your right foot.

only *once*. Be sure to bring your arm back as soon as you've made this signal. Remember that your hand signal lasts only as long as the verbal command.

If your dog doesn't go Down at your command, take a step toward him with your left foot. Your step should cover about half the distance between the two of you. You should start heading toward your dog, making that step with your left foot, as soon as you finish your verbal command and hand signal.

After stepping toward him, slowly bring your right foot up and use it to press on the leash, just as you did when you corrected your dog's Down from the side.

Remember again *not* to press the leash all the way to the ground. As soon as you've tapped the leash, place your right foot back on the ground where it was before you raised it and wait for about three seconds, giving your dog the chance to go Down. If he doesn't, press on the leash again with your right foot and remove it. Try to correct your dog in this way without too much pressure.

As soon as he goes Down, slowly step all the way back to the end of your leash, where you were standing when you first gave him the Down command, and praise him calmly with verbal praise.

Be sure not to move away from your dog too quickly after you've corrected him though. A fast motion on your part might make him rise. Pulling on the leash when you step back might also make him rise—you want to be sure that you maintain a slack line. If your dog does start to get up, try to stop him by pressing with your right foot. If he gets too far up for that maneuver to be effective, put him back into a Sit by sliding your right hand halfway up the leash to stop him from coming forward. Once you have him in the Sit, press on the leash with your right foot again to put him back into the Down position. Do not repeat your command.

By this time your dog should be familiar with the foot-on-leash correction. However if he still has trouble with Down from the front after you've tried a few times, you may want to return to the Heel position, standing at his side, and Down him a few times from there. After that, try the Down from the front again.

If he still resists you can also place your right hand behind his shoulders and press there as you make the correction with your right foot.

Remember when he does go Down you should step all the way back to the end of your leash and verbally praise him—*calmly*.

"Sit" from the Front

To get your dog to Sit when he is in the Down position in front of you, make a signal with your right hand—a sharp upward arc as though you were pitching a softball underhanded—as you say "Sit."

Start your "Sit" signal as if you were pitching a softball underhanded.

Give the "Sit" command.

If he doesn't Sit on his own, step in toward him—this time with your right foot first. At the same time you step forward, slide your right hand along the leash as you move it upward, holding it above his head, and using it to make light snaps on his collar.

You want to start with a light snap then lift him by increments, little by little, until he is in the Sit position.

Just like the foot-on-leash correction, your dog should be familiar with these upward leash corrections since you used them while getting him to Sit from the Down at your side. When you have your dog in the Sit position, Break him.

To correct, step forward right foot first.

Hold your leash upward and make light snaps on the collar.

Daisy.

[CHAPTER 13]

"Don't Touch"

IIIIIIIIII

WOULDN'T IT BE NICE IF YOU COULD GIVE YOUR DOG one command when someone is entering your house or yard and have him turn away from that person? Not even show any interest in them if they called him? Or wouldn't it be nice if you could teach your dog not to snatch food from a child? Or not to snatch a sandwich off the kitchen counter? This command, "Don't Touch," is one of my favorite commands, and it can be used with your dog to refer to anyone or anything.

What "Don't Touch" Means

When you tell your dog "Don't Touch," it means more than "you just can't touch that." It actually means "turn away and don't show any more interest in that." When you give your dog this command you should expect him to literally turn his head away from the object you're designating.

Teaching Your Dog "Don't Touch"

To teach your dog this command you'll need to recruit a helper, preferably not a family member. This person will hold a piece of food your dog desires in his closed hand. You will stand, holding your leash, with your dog on Break. The helper will then approach your dog and reach out with that closed hand to tempt him. As soon as you see your dog show interest in the helper's hand (and, of course, the food it contains) and start heading in that direction, say, "Don't Touch!" You'll want to give this command just before your dog makes contact.

Have a helper approach with food.

When you give the command you should also be sure to speak in a sharp, clear tone and emphasize the "touch" word, with its sharper sound.

Then step back—be sure to step back—and make a quick snap on your dog's chain, heading him off at an angle, to the right or the left, so that he must turn and walk away from your helper's offered hand. If your dog doesn't turn—if he keeps focusing on the hand even when backing away—repeat your snaps on his collar until he actually turns his head away. Then give him a pat on the back to balance the correction.

Step back and make a quick snap on your dog's chain.

Have your helper approach again, and repeat your command and corrections. Take a step backward with every snap until your dog turns away.

You are looking for your dog to *turn away* on your command, "Don't Touch!" without having to give any snaps on his collar at all. When that happens give your dog verbal and hand praise.

When your dog has turned away on your command three or four times consecutively, the next step is to have your helper approach while you refrain from giving the command.

Your dog should turn away.

If your dog shows interest in your helper's offered hand at this point, step back and correct him without giving the verbal command first. Do this until he turns away on his own when your helper reaches out. In this way you're teaching your dog that one command—Don't Touch—means "don't touch and don't go back to that object."

At first you should practice this command with your dog while he's on-leash. Try using it on various objects he might have an interest in sniffing until you see that he will turn away consistently on one command from you. Then you can try giving him the command while he's off-leash.

What Is Meant By a Temporary and a Permanent "Don't Touch"?

There are two ways of using the Don't Touch lesson you've taught your dog. One has to do with your use of the verbal command that signifies a temporary Don't Touch. The other has to do with things you *never* want your dog to touch. These things are a permanent Don't Touch and don't involve a verbal command. You need to decide for yourself which things in your life should not need your verbal command to ensure that your dog will not approach them in the first place.

Remember the earlier reference to the sandwich on the kitchen counter? Let's say you leave your sandwich there while you go to another room to get something. If your dog is in the kitchen in your absence would you want him to completely resist going after that sandwich, or would you want him to resist only if you took the trouble to tell him "Don't Touch"?

If you feel you should tell him "Don't Touch," that would make your command a temporary command, and he could go ahead and take the sandwich any time he wanted unless you were there to tell him otherwise.

If, on the other hand, you never want him taking your sandwich, or probably any food off the counter, you would make all objects on the counter a permanent Don't Touch. To do so, you would give an automatic correction—a snap of the collar—away from the object as soon as your dog showed interest in it. A permanent Don't Touch could refer to socks, cats, food in a child's hand, any object you never want your dog to go after on his own.

Another use of the permanent Don't Touch could involve other people. I do not want my dog to go up to other people on his own, so I make all people other than the family a permanent Don't Touch. This eliminates a lot of problems. I can walk in public places, around a group of strangers, and my dog will not reach out to sniff or make contact with any of them. If you want to work on this with your dog, have people other than family squat down and call him over to them. As he attempts to go to them, make an automatic correction *without* giving him the Don't Touch command.

An exception to this situation involves your dog when he is in his own territory. You should not expect your dog not to touch someone who is approaching his territory. There is such a strong inclination for him to make contact with anyone new coming into his home or yard that in this case I don't expect my dog to follow the permanent Don't Touch restriction without my command. Even though I expect people to be a permanent Don't Touch, not requiring a verbal command for him to avoid them, I give him a Don't Touch command at home. This means he gets the command on his territory but not when we are away from his territory.

If Your Dog Disobeys a Permanent Don't Touch

If your dog disobeys a permanent Don't Touch and you don't "catch him in the act," you should still correct him. Back to the sandwich example: let's say you've already made objects on the kitchen counter a permanent Don't Touch—by making an automatic correction whenever your dog showed inter-

Take your dog back to the place where he made his mistake.

Then snap him away from the person or object.

est in them—and you return to find that your sandwich has been eaten by your dog. Even though the incident has already happened, you should bring your dog back up to the site of his crime, in this case the place on the counter where the sandwich was, and snap him away.

You can put on your leash if need be to help with the correction.

> *Do not let your dog get away without the correction, even though the mistake was made when you weren't there.*

The same principle goes for other permanent Don't Touch objects—such as people. If your dog runs up to someone and then moves away, you should take him back to that person—in other words, back to the place where he made his mistake—and then snap him away.

You want to show him that each time he disobeys he will receive a correction, and that you always expect him to obey your rules.

Overriding a Permanent "Don't Touch"

You may have taught your dog a permanent Don't Touch and then decided that you want to temporarily permit him to touch that object. For example, other dogs may be a permanent Don't Touch, but you might decide that your dog can make contact with a friend's dog. Or other people may be a permanent Don't Touch, but you decide that someone can meet/pet your dog. In these cases you can erase your previous command by bringing your dog up to the object you've decided he can touch. For instance where people are concerned, you could say "Make Friends" as you bring your dog up to them. I want to make it clear to my dog that I am giving him permission to make this contact. *I've decided when it's OK; I haven't allowed him to decide and to pull me toward whatever object may have interested him.*

"Take It"

"Take It" means "pick it up." I like to use the "Take It" command for objects I may have told my dog not to touch and now want him to have. This command could refer to such things as a ball, a bone, or food. To teach this command to your dog a good way to begin is with his food bowl. Every time you set his food down, say "Take It" just as he goes for it. When he starts to pick up his ball or bone, say "Take It." In this way you'll condition him to associate the command with literally taking an object. After several days of this conditioning, give him a Don't Touch command when you put his food down. Be ready to correct him with a quick snap away if he starts to go for the bowl in spite of your command. Then in a softer voice say "Take It," and bump the food with your hand. The very moment he starts to look at the food praise him and walk away.

"Drop"

Another basic command you should teach your dog is "Drop." This means "Let go of whatever you have in your mouth," and it can be very handy in a number of situations.

I was driving down a road one day and saw two kids walking a husky. I noticed one of them kicking the dog. He had a squirrel in his mouth and the kids couldn't even begin to get him to release it. I stopped and asked if they would like some help from a dog trainer. The dog was wearing a nylon collar and had a death grip on the squirrel. I told the little girl that I was going to tighten up on the collar to put pressure on the dog's throat so that he would have to open his mouth to take a breath and would then drop the squirrel. I told her the whole process would most likely take about thirty seconds. It did.

My German shepherds like to play ball. If you throw a ball, a lot of dogs will go after it, but they don't want to bring it back, because they've learned you will take it from them. When my dog starts to pick up the ball I say, "Take It." When he comes close to me with the ball, instead of reaching for it I give him a pat on the back. I want him to feel comfortable being close to me with the ball in his mouth. When I feel he isn't concerned about being close to me with the ball in his mouth, and loves getting the praise, I take hold of his collar and tighten it from the back of his neck as I say, "Drop." When he drops it I praise him and throw it for him again, repeating the process several times.

It's important to note that when you tighten the collar to get your dog to let go of something in his mouth, you don't tighten and then release the collar before he releases the object in his mouth. If you release the collar—even for a second—he will be able to regain his breath and not be forced to drop the object. And you will be forced to start the process over again. Instead you must keep pres-

Tighten your dog's collar.

Praise him as he drops the object.

sure on him until he drops it, then praise him.

If you follow through with this approach you'll notice that each time you give the Drop command and tighten his collar, he will drop the object sooner. Eventually he'll drop it entirely on your command, without you having to tighten his collar at all.

Once your dog understands the Drop command, you can start making an automatic correction for items you never want him to pick up in the first place—permanent Don't Touch items. If he takes your shoe, for instance, simply make the collar-tightening correction to make him release it without giving him the Drop command. Why should you have to tell him to drop something he never should have picked up in the first place?

Zeus.

[CHAPTER 14]

The Patrol Position

IF YOU GET NOTHING ELSE FROM THIS BOOK, THE Patrol position—what we consider the third way of walking with your dog—would be well worth it. It's easier to show your dog this position after he's learned the Heel, though it's definitely not necessary to learn the Heel first.

Advantages of the Patrol Position

The advantage of using this position is to have your dog walking close to you without pulling or jumping. In the Patrol position you can walk with your dog hassle-free and yet have complete control over him. Another way to look at it is that with this position you can walk as comfortably with your dog as you would without him.

Standing in the Patrol position.

In the Heel position your dog must keep his eye on you, but having your dog keep his eye on you all the time is just not practical. When you're out for a walk with your dog do you think your dog wants to watch you constantly? Do you want to have to watch him? Why not allow him to look around and enjoy the walk?

Or think about walking into a veterinary clinic with your dog. Would you want to walk in on a Break or on a Heel? With the Break your dog can be six feet from you, and with the Heel you must constantly keep your eye on him. By walking in with your dog in the Patrol position you can have your dog completely under control while only using your left hand. This method leaves your right hand free to open the door, sign in, or whatever.

I've actually seen some police officers give their dogs a Heel command to walk them to the beginning of a track or out to make contact with someone. In these cases the Heel is not appropriate. There is no way these dogs are going to look only at their handlers because they are focused, and should be, on the scene. Being walked in a Patrol position, on the other hand, would allow the dog to focus on his surroundings and still provide the officer with control over his dog. It would also allow the officer to take his eyes off his dog and observe other things himself.

Hold an approaching person back with your right hand.

This position can be invaluable for you when you're walking down a crowded street. It's really nice to be in full control of your dog in these instances so that he doesn't make contact with people or things, and people don't make contact with him.

For example if someone reaches out to pet your dog, you're able to hold him back with your left hand while stepping forward with your right arm extended. In this way you prevent the person from making contact while you explain to them that your dog is in training, and it's a good idea to ask first before petting him. If you decide that it's all right for them to pet your dog then you can bring him up to them and give him a cue that you are overriding the permanent Don't Touch. This is where a phrase like "Make Friends," comes in handy.

> *Remember:* You *make the decisions about who will have contact with your dog—not your dog, and certainly not other people.*

Differences between the Patrol Position and the Heel Position

When I'm using the Patrol position, most people would look at my dog walking at my left side and think the dog was Heeling. I can see why. Just as with the Heel, in the Patrol position your dog must walk at your left side. However there are some very important differences between these positions.

Notice the leash in the illustrations. When you are on a Heel you should have about four feet of slack in your leash; you want a loose leash so you can make effective corrections. On a Patrol you have a tight, taut leash.

Think about the difference it makes whether you have a *slack* leash or a *taut* one. When you are on a Heel and have a slack leash your dog is forced to watch you. If he doesn't, you may make a turn, hesitate, or side step, and his lack of attention would result in a correction for him. Through your maneuvers you would force him to keep his eye on you. With a short, tight leash he doesn't have to watch

The Patrol position. *The Heel position.*

you to know where you are. He can feel it. And you don't have to watch him. As you can see in the of the Patrol position, she's walking as she would if she were walking without a dog.

When you walk in the Patrol position your dog can have his head slightly in front of you and be able to explore what's ahead. When you turn, slow down, or stop he will feel a small amount of tension on his collar and must follow the direction of your leash. It's a little bit like steering a horse by moving the reins in one direction or another.

Getting into the Patrol Position

There is no command to get your dog into the Patrol position. The positioning involved is done by you.

As with the Heel position, it's very important that you hold your leash correctly; however this time you'll be using a very different approach.

To get into the Patrol position, first slide your left hand down the leash. Next lock your left thumb in the leash loop.

Slide your left hand down the leash.

Place the loop of the leash over your left thumb.

Next make another loop of your leash—this will be above your leash clip. The distance between this second loop and the clip will depend on the height of your dog. In this example the distance of the second loop is about eight inches from the leash clip.

Once you have the second loop, place that loop over the first one.

When you have the double loop in your left hand, lock it all together by closing your left hand. If you have followed this process as described, the second loop of the leash will be OVER the first loop.

Make another loop of your leash.

Place this loop over the first.

Lock all together by closing your left hand.

As you walk with your dog in this position you want to be in a relaxed stance with your arm comfortably at your side.

If you have short arms and/or a small dog, you will need to let out some of your leash to make this happen. If you have long arms and/or a taller dog, holding the leash about six inches from the clip should be about right.

How to Walk with Your Dog in the Patrol Position

Once you have your leash properly positioned, you can simply start moving forward. Try not to look at your dog as you walk with him. Remember, not having to look at your dog is one of the benefits of walking in the Patrol position. However, you do want to be conscious of where he is (which you should be able to know with your eyes closed) since your dog's shoulders should not pass your torso. If he's pulling ahead and starting to pass, you may need to make a correction.

Think back to working with your dog on Break. When your dog got to the end of his leash, that didn't necessarily mean it was time to correct him with a snap on the collar. You made your correction only when he was pulling *hard enough* to warrant a correction. If you became aware of how much pull was too much and consistently corrected at that point, your dog came to know if he pulled that hard he would trigger a correction.

You need to correct if your dog is pulling too hard or starting to pass you.

The same principle applies here. Your correction when in the Patrol position will be a sharp snap in the opposite direction of his pull. In other words, if he's forging ahead of you, you'll make a sharp snap backward. As you walk with your dog, try to hold your arm vertically near your left leg so that you have space to release the tension of the leash and make that correction on the dog's collar.

If you find that your corrections aren't effective in stopping his pull, you might use both hands to correct with a snap or bring his collar up just below his ears, or use a prong collar for several days, then try going back to the choke chain.

Another difference between this position and the Heel is that when you stop, your dog doesn't have to sit. But that doesn't mean that when you stop he can forge ahead of you. To

Correct with a sharp snap in the opposite direction.

prevent this from happening, keep your leash hand back slightly, toward your thigh, as you come to a stop. Don't let your dog's shoulders pass your legs and don't let him turn around and face you.

If your dog wants to sit at your side when you stop, it's fine. And if he wants to lie there, you can let out some of the slack of your leash to enable him to do so.

Just be sure that when he stands, you pick up the slack you released. If he starts to crawl forward when he's lying down, bend down, give a quick snap on his collar in the direction of his tail, and then immediately stand up.

Always, whenever you're in the Patrol position, be sure to keep your thumb locked around both loops of your leash. And remember: there's no command to get your dog into the Patrol position. He will know when you start positioning your leash.

Your dog may sit or lie at your side.

Champ.

[CHAPTER 15]

Off-Leash Come and the Chase Game

UP TO THIS POINT IN YOUR TRAINING YOU MAY HAVE spent about two to three weeks showing your dog the learning phase for each lesson, applying corrections when necessary, and practicing with him on a regular basis. If you have done so and are confident that you and your dog can perform the previous lessons well on a consistent basis, you've created a solid foundation in training your dog on-leash. Now it's time to take off your leash and let your dog run free so that you can teach him to come back to you on your first command when he's off-leash.

Tools You'll Need

By now your dog should be familiar with the Come command when he's on-leash, so it will be easy for you to teach him what the command means when he's off-leash.

Easy with one exception—since he has four legs, he's faster that you are. You'll need to start your lesson in a fenced area, and you'll need the help of a few items.

Tab

This is a much shorter version of your dog's leash. Having it on him will help you get control of his chain if you need to correct him. To make a tab, take a lightweight leash, tie a knot in it about three or four inches from the leash clip, and cut the long part of the leash off. Burn the end of the knot with a match so that it doesn't fray.

Different sizes of tabs.

The length and weight of the tab will depend on the size of your dog. A stronger tab is more appropriate for a large dog and a lighter one for a smaller dog. You should easily be able to grasp your tab in one hand, and your dog should feel as if he has no leash on at all.

Correct if your dog chews on the tab.

If your dog tries to chew on his tab, give the Don't Touch command, and be ready to correct him. Because you cannot tug a dog away from the tab while he is wearing it, I tug the tab into my dog.

As with all your training, the difference between making this correction work or not will be your *timing*. Just as your dog goes for the tab, you go for it. Give a quick snap with the tab toward his nose and then walk away, watching out the corner of your eye for his next attempt and your next correction.

> *To stop his undesirable behavior you must be more consistent with your corrections than your dog is with his unwanted behavior.*

Throw Chains

You will need at least two extra chains; you can use old choke collars as throw chains. They will be critical in teaching your dog not to run from you. The chains should be about twenty inches long and about the same weight as the chain your dog is wearing—the smaller the dog, the lighter the chain.

Different weights of throw chains.

Teaching Your Dog to Come to You Off-Leash

Praise your dog as he approaches you.

As you begin this lesson, have one throw chain in your pocket and one in your right hand. Turn your dog loose in the fenced area you've chosen, and give him a minute or two to walk around free.

Since he's off-leash and his mind is likely off you, you should use his name first to get his attention when you call him, although you only want to use it *once*. As in "Jake," followed by a slight, one-second pause, then "Come."

Use your hand signal as you command him in case he looks up at you.

Give him one second to turn and start coming toward you; and if he does, squat down and give him verbal praise all the time he's approaching you.

If He Comes to You on Your Command

Once he arrives, give him a lot of hand and verbal praise, and then immediately give him the Break command.

In this instance he is not required to sit in front of you since you are "interrupting his Sit" with your squatting position and the all hand praise. You want him to know that when he comes to you he is going to get lots of praise and get to go free again. This reception on your part should motivate him to want to come to you when you call.

Give a lot of hand and verbal praise when he Comes.

If He Doesn't Come to You

If your dog doesn't start toward you within a second of your calling him, go after him. As you take off, shuffle your feet on gravel or stomp on the ground so that even if his back is turned to you, he'll know you're coming after him. You want him to know that at that moment you've already started a correction.

Now could be the start of the "chase game." If your dog turns his back and starts to run away from you as you approach him, launch a throw chain toward his hind end with an underhand throw. Since you are already holding that chain in your right hand, you should be prepared to toss it in a timely manner—just when he turns his back on you and starts to take off.

It's fine if the throw chain hits your dog's hind end, his back feet, or the ground behind him. If it hits him it won't hurt him, but it will be slightly uncomfortable and may deter him from running farther. It should be as if the impact of the throw chain is an extension of your arm—as if your arm magically extended and reached your dog.

Launch a throw chain if your dog runs from you.

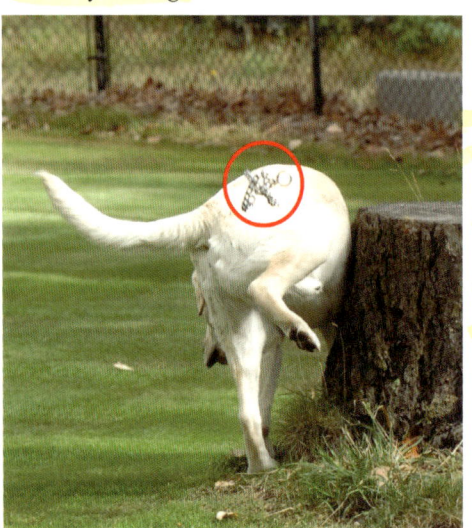

The chain can reach him from a distance.

You want him to know that even if he isn't leashed, you can still reach him from a distance. Getting him to believe this is another huge breaking point in having control over him.

The most important thing to remember in using this technique is to get the next chain (the one you kept in your pocket) in your hand, ready to launch if he turns his back again. You may even need to "leapfrog" the chains, tossing one, then the other, picking up the first one and getting ready to toss it again. You need to keep this going—moving after your dog and tossing the chains at his rear—until he decides he has had enough and it looks like he wants to stop running.

At that point you should approach him slowly so that you don't appear to be a big threat. It's very important to approach him slowly when he's facing you, and have a chain ready to launch if he turns his back on you. He should hear a chain coming at him every time he turns to run, but you should never throw the chain at him when he's looking at you!

As you approach your dog, keep verbal praise going—"good boy, good boy"—and reach for him with your left hand. Grab the tab attached to his collar and keep him on your left side as you run back to the spot where you stood when you first called him.

When you run him back, use your tab to tighten-release, tighten-release his collar. You want him to know you are in control, that you are taking him back. You don't want to let him drag you back.

Grab the tab and keep him on your left side.

Tighten–release, tighten–release as you bring him back.

Once you've returned to the spot where you started, turn so that you're facing the same direction you faced when you called him, and bring your dog into a Sit directly in front of you.

This is where he should have arrived had he responded correctly to your Come command in the first place. Give him hand praise and then Break him.

Bring your dog into a Sit in front of you.

Be sure to release your dog after he Comes.

At this point people often make the mistake of not turning their dogs loose again. When they do that they are not giving their dogs the chance to learn this lesson. Your dog needs to know that you will run him down effectively and bring him back whenever you call.

In teaching him this lesson you want to show your dog that he can come to you and you will rub him up and let him go again. Eventually he'll come running to you knowing that his return doesn't have to mean confinement. Instead he can get praise and be set free again.

After you release him, give your dog the chance to wander again and then call him. Repeat the procedure you just followed if he doesn't come. If he's been running from you and you've had to use your throw chains, watch to see if he turns and seems to think about coming to you. At that very moment, you should squat down and start to praise him as he begins to come toward you. Give him verbal praise all the time he's moving in the direction you want. Then, when he reaches you, "rub him up" with lots of hand praise, and Break him. Remember: don't make your dog sit if he comes to you on his own.

If you have to go after your dog to bring him to you, then you should make him Sit in front of you. This rule also applies if your dog starts to come to you and then veers off, moving past you or away from you, or if he stops en route and doesn't come all the way to you. In each of those cases you would have to approach him, grab his tab, and bring him to you; and in each of those cases, you should make him Sit in front before you Break him.

Once your dog comes to you on your first command three or four times, end your workout. To build your effectiveness with this command, in future workouts stand near his kennel, or some other place you know he'd rather not go. When you call him he might think you're calling to put him into the kennel. Or he might be outdoors and not want to come in. If you stand by the door and call him, he may think you're calling to make him come indoors. In any of these instances if he doesn't come when you call, go get him, bring him to the spot where you were when you called, praise him, and Break him. Repeat this until he comes to you once or twice without your having to get him. You want to show him that coming to you doesn't necessarily mean that something negative—for example, having to go into the kennel—will occur.

Captain.

[CHAPTER 16]

Temporary Boundaries

||||||||||

BOUNDARIES CAN MAKE A VERY BIG DIFFERENCE IN living with your dog. I'd like to remind you of a situation mentioned earlier in the lesson on Stay because I think it's so important. When I asked people what they told their dogs when they didn't want them to get out of the car, their answer was the same as it would be if they wanted their dogs to sit perfectly still in one spot: "Stay." Most people don't realize that they confuse their dogs by giving one command yet expecting two entirely different behaviors. For this reason, clarifying what you are actually telling your dog, before trying to teach him boundaries, is invaluable.

What is a Temporary Boundary?

A temporary boundary is a line you don't want your dog to cross at a particular moment. As an example, let's say that normally your dog can enter and exit the kitchen when he wants. But if you break a glass on your kitchen floor and want to keep your dog out of the area while you clean it up, you could make the doorway to the kitchen a temporary boundary for him.

When you designate a temporary boundary, you're telling your dog you don't want him going any farther in the direction he's heading. You give him a command, "Stay Back," to stop him from moving ahead. Your command means "do not cross this line." It doesn't mean he has to stand still; he can move around on the acceptable side of the line. He just can't cross the line until you either call him across it or free him from your Stay Back command by giving him the Break command. For instance, with the kitchen example above, after the broken glass has been cleared away, you could say "Break," and allow your dog access to the room.

Teaching Your Dog the "Stay Back" Command

In order to teach this concept to your dog, it's helpful to find a clearly identifiable opening such as a doorway, a gate, or something similar that will designate a boundary. A surface that makes a clear transition from one substance to another, such as linoleum to carpet, or concrete to grass, could also work. In the beginning stages of teaching this new command you want to make the boundary, whatever it is you choose, easy for your dog to recognize.

After you've found the boundary you want to use, have your dog Heel and walk in and out of the entrance you've chosen. Make Right–Abouts and Left Turns as you go back and forth so you can be sure the dog is focused on you, and not focused on forging ahead through the doorway or entrance. When you feel you have his attention you're ready to start the learning phase of this command.

1. Signaling

There are three steps to take in signaling your dog that he's to stop before he crosses the boundary: a hand signal, a verbal command, and a pivot.

As mentioned, only when you're satisfied that you have your dog's attention, approach the doorway with the dog on a Heel and signal the boundary by drawing a line with your left hand just at the edge of the door opening. To make this hand signal, sweep your left hand in an arc from top to bottom, in front of your dog. The back of your hand should face your dog as your palm faces forward.

As you make this hand signal, give

Signal the boundary with your left hand.   *Pivot as you say, "Stay Back."*

the verbal command, "Stay Back," and pivot on your left foot so that your right foot is stepping in front of the dog.

A successful pivot/step should find you standing directly in front of your dog. In this way you can help the dog stop before he crosses the line by blocking him with your body.

2. Back Up

The next step is to back up very slowly, crossing the boundary line yourself, while facing him—but don't back up all the way to the end of your leash on the first try. This maneuver is similar to what you did when you taught your dog the Stay. You should also switch thumbs so your left thumb is in the leash loop, and your right hand is on the leash.

Stand directly in front of your dog.

Back up while facing your dog.

3. Correction

If your dog steps over the boundary line, stop him by sliding your right hand up the leash the same way you would if you were correcting him for moving out of a Stay position. A big difference in your leash angle, though, is that you don't snap the leash upward to place him in the Sit position. Instead you give a tug to the right or the left. You don't want the dog to think you're trying to get him to Sit and Stay; you only want to show him that he can't cross the line.

Timing is critical. You must start your correction just when his paw steps over the line, no earlier. And you must end your correction just when he's back on the correct side of the line, no later. Tighten the collar just as he steps over the line and loosen it just as he falls back. Once he is on the other side of the line you need to turn off your correction with your body language.

If your dog completely crosses over the line, run him back and release your slack just as he falls on the other side of the line. Don't cross the line with him. You remain on the side you were on. He goes back to the side where he was to remain.

Correct with a tug to the right or left.

4. Break

The first time you try to teach this to your dog, get him to stay inside the line for only a few seconds before you give him the Break command and back up, thereby allowing him to cross the line and come over to your side. If he doesn't cross when you Break him, give him a tug.

5. Repeat

After you Break your dog, praise him, and repeat the procedure by starting with the Heel command, going back through the doorway, and turning around to approach the boundary from the direction you took the first time. Again signal, give the "Stay Back" command at the boundary, pivot, and see if your dog will stop before he crosses the line. Wait a second or two, then Break him.

For most dogs it takes about a half-dozen attempts before they will stop at the line without the need for a correction. This is the case unless you're really good with your body language when you make that pivot. When your dog *does* manage to stop at the line and doesn't cross it, praise him verbally, quietly and slowly so as not to excite him too much, then Break him and really, really praise him—both verbally and with lots of hand praise.

You should probably end your training session at this point and try again at the end of the day, or the following day. When you do resume this lesson the next step would be to have your dog Stay Back for a longer time period—say ten or fifteen seconds—before you Break him and let him cross the line. Remember that he can sniff the ground or move around on his side of the boundary as long as he doesn't cross that boundary line.

Really praise your dog after you Break him.

Teaching Temporary Boundaries with the "Stay Back" Command

Once your dog understands the Stay Back, command you should teach him to respond to it in different situations and in different ways. Your next step would be to reverse direction so that you approach the doorway boundary from the opposite side, and have your dog Stay Back on that side. Then walk back and forth through the doorway with him on a Heel and vary which side of the boundary you use

when you tell him to Stay Back. In this way you stop him from anticipating when you are going to give the command and encourage his attention on you.

When you can see that your dog is following the command, tell him to Stay Back, back up, drop the leash when you get to the end of it, and slowly move several feet back from the leash. If your dog doesn't cross the boundary, walk toward him in a non-threatening way, cross over to his side of the line, and as you pass him, give him a pat on the shoulder or back.

Give your dog a pat as you walk past him.

Your intent is to get him to turn and follow you so that he can see it's all right to move around on that side of the line. Remember he can move around, sniff the ground, sit, lie down, or whatever; he just can't cross the boundary you designated when you told him to Stay Back.

Immediately after you pass and pat him, turn around and head back through the doorway. Don't stare at your dog, but watch him out of the corner of your eye, over your shoulder, so that you can charge him if he crosses the line to follow you. As mentioned before, your timing is very important. Try to start a quick movement toward him the second his paw steps over the line.

With this exercise you show your dog that you can give him a command to stay out of a room or any other designated area. While you yourself can move back and forth, in and out of that space, he can only move around on his own side of the boundary line.

If your dog should cross the line you've designated, and then back up on his own when he sees you heading for him, don't let him get by without being corrected. Tug him back to the spot he reached when he crossed over the boundary and then run him back across the line where he should have stayed in the first place. It's very important that you show

Bring him back to the spot where he made his mistake.   *Run him back across the boundary.*

him he has to obey when you tell him to Stay Back, not just when he sees he's been "caught in the act of misbehaving."

If you need to correct your dog for crossing the line, be sure to turn your back to him as soon as you've released him on the correct side of the boundary line.

> *Remember, when you end a correction can be as important as when you start a correction. It helps clarify for your dog exactly when he made his mistake.*

Turn from your dog right away, but, again, watch out of the corner of your eye to see if he will Stay Back. Be sure you're ready to make another quick correction if he doesn't.

When your dog is following your Stay Back command in this situation, Break him, and as you give the Break command, step backward. With your body language you'll be helping him understand that he can cross the line and head in your direction. If he doesn't cross immediately, grab the leash and tug it lightly so that he'll come across the line.

Turn your back immediately after your correction.

Practicing "Stay Back"

At this point you should practice temporary boundaries using many different openings or surfaces to designate your boundary line. You could also work with wider openings such as a garage door. For example, have your dog stay in or out of the garage for several minutes while you move around on the other side of the designated boundary.

You can build your dog's ability to respond to this command by setting up distractions, like a person walking by, that could tempt him to cross the boundary lines. By correcting him in a timely manner if he makes a mistake, you can teach him to overcome his desire to respond to the distraction.

Set up distractions to build your dog's ability to Stay Back.

Build the length of time you ask your dog to Stay Back, but be sure to Break your dog so he knows how long he's expected to wait before he can cross the line. And be sure you don't forget you set that boundary.

A friend who lives on a three-hundred-acre ranch told me recently that years ago when he went through this training with me he taught his dog that the back of his pickup truck was a boundary the dog could cross only on command. One day after he came home with his dog and left him in the truck, a friend pulled up and they left together to spend some time at the friend's place. He forgot about leaving his dog in the truck until he came back and found him there several hours later.

Using "Stay Back" from a Distance

Now you're going to try something different. Using a doorway or a gate, leave your dog about ten feet from the opening by telling him, "Sit, Stay." Go through the doorway and stop about five feet from your side of the opening. Face your dog, and then call him to you with "Come."

Call your dog to you. *Step forward to reinforce the "Stay Back" command.*

As he approaches the doorway, and when he still has time to stop before passing through the doorway, give him a verbal Stay Back command. Don't make a hand signal, but do use body language by taking one abrupt step toward him to help show him that he's to stop.

If your dog makes a mistake and crosses the line, the second he does so run him back to the other side, Break him, and then try again. Remember not to cross the line with him if you have to run him back. If he does stop at your command, Break him right away as you take a step backward, and then praise the "you know what" out of him.

Rocco.

[CHAPTER 17]

Permanent Boundaries

AFTER YOU HAVE TAUGHT YOUR DOG WHAT A TEMPORARY boundary is, you can start establishing permanent boundaries.

What Is a Permanent Boundary?

Permanent boundaries are boundaries, or lines of demarcation, that you never want your dog to cross on his own. While you give the Stay Back command to tell your dog not to cross a temporary boundary, you give no command if your dog is *never* to cross a permanent boundary—a line you don't want him to cross even if you aren't around, or even if you aren't giving a verbal order to Stay Back.

The Car as a Permanent Boundary

Going to the car example mentioned earlier, when I ask what command you would give your dog to make sure he stays put when you open the car door, your answer should be, "None." Your car should be a permanent boundary in both directions so that your dog only enters at your command and only exits at your command. No matter which side he's on—either in the car or out of it—he should not cross the boundary of that car door without your permission.

The car is actually a great place to start teaching your dog the concept of permanent boundaries, since it's usually a place he may be very eager to either enter or exit. If you're prepared, leash in hand, you have the opportunity to make a quick correction and really clarify this lesson for your dog.

Be ready if your dog starts to enter the car on his own.

As you approach your car and open the door, you should be ready in case your dog decides to jump in on his own without your permission. Observe him very carefully and if this happens, be prepared to give a quick snap on his collar just when his toe crosses the line into the car. Make sure you correct just at that moment—no sooner. Your goal is to stop him right when he tries to get into the car.

Once he's stopped trying to get in on his own, give him a command to enter the car. I use the word "In" to indicate anything I want my dog to enter, such as "In the car," "In the crate," "In the kennel," "In your room," and so on. Remember to give him your command only once.

If he doesn't jump in right away, make him get in by tightening and releasing his leash and collar in the direction of the car. Each time you tug toward the car you should move your dog at least six inches closer to entering. Do not lift his body and place him into the car. Make him use his own back legs to get himself in or he will depend on you to lift him in.

Once you know he's on his way back in with the help of your correction, *stop* your correction so he will know that what he is doing at that time (being in the car) is right.

When your dog is in the car, watch for him to try to exit on his own. Be ready to catch him with a quick leash correc-

Tighten and release the leash and collar to get your dog into the car.

tion just as his paw starts over the sill of the door. Be sure you say nothing. Not "Stay," not "No," not "Back in." Nothing. Just make your correction, step back, and wait. Watch for him to make another move but don't stare at him. If you stare at him he will see that he has your attention and may think he's still doing something wrong. In other words, in his mind he would still be getting corrected.

> As with all your corrections, it's very important that you know when to turn the correction on and when to turn it off.

Wait until your dog shows that he's not going to step out of the car on his own, then give him a Come command. If he then jumps out, give him lots of praise.

If he doesn't jump out, tug him out by backing up and making him move toward you about a foot at a time.

Be sure to send him in and call him out of the car enough times in one session until he enters and exits on your command without your having to use your leash to force him in either direction.

Give the "Come" command to have your dog exit the car.

Reinforcing the Car as a Permanent Boundary

When you are dealing with an intelligent, thinking animal such as a dog, you may find that if you leave your car door open and go out of his sight, he may decide to jump out on his own to go find you. Set him up for this situation by leaving the door open and moving from the car to a spot where he can't see you. Be sure that you don't move too far away, since the moment your dog steps out of the car you should charge him. If you can, let him know you're on your way by letting him hear the sound of your feet as you head for him. When he hears you it's likely he'll run back and jump into the car.

In this instance if you stop yourself from correcting him because you think he has corrected himself, you would be making a big mistake. By your response he would learn that all he has to do to avoid correction is run from you and go back into the car. When you try to correct him the next time, it would be the start of the same game. Remember: just as you didn't let him get away without a correction where crossing temporary boundaries was concerned, you can't let him get away without a correction here. You must correct your dog even if he runs back into the car before you reach him.

Charge after your dog if he gets out on his own.

Recreate your dog's mistake if he enters without your permission.

Go to the car, get him, and run him out of the car back to the spot he reached when he exited on his own. In other words, recreate what he just did. Then correct him back into the car.

The type of correction you make here depends on your dog. If he's running back into the car on his own, he's probably worried about your reaction. Congratulations. You are now becoming your dog's leader. Since he's concerned about your correction, go light on the correction. The same rule applies in other situations where you see that he's worried about being corrected.

However, if you see that your dog could care less about your reaction, that's when you need to step things up. As you run him back to the car, tighten the choke with the knot of your tab and, depending on how far your dog is from the car, tighten and release, tighten and release, over and over, until you are about six feet from the door. At this point tighten the choke until he's on his way into the car. The moment you know he's entering the car, release the tab, turn your back to him, and walk away. The correction is over.

Establishing Other Permanent Boundaries

First decide where you want to establish permanent boundaries—then let your dog know where the permanent boundaries are by enforcing your restrictions. To do this you need to make the same correction you would make if he crossed a temporary boundary—a quick tug back across the line—whenever he crosses the permanent boundary on his own. Again the big difference here is that here you aren't giving him any verbal command. Your actions are speaking for you.

Jumping on people can be considered a violation of a permanent boundary. If you did not tell your dog to get on something in the first place and would like to keep it that way—for example, if you never told him to jump on you and don't want him to do so—then don't tell him to get off, just correct him.

Physical boundaries can be specific to your own situation. For example I've set up all the gates in my back yard as permanent boundaries because I often go in and out of them, and I know my dog would like to go with me even when I don't want him to do so. I also don't want to have to give him a command every time I pass through a gate. He knows that the gates are permanent boundaries because he knows that if he were to exit through any of them I would correct him.

Unlike the car, though, my gates are not permanent boundaries in both directions. They're only permanent boundaries for my dog if he's going out of them. This means he can go back into my yard any time he wants. Once he's back inside though, he can't cross through the gates again without my permission.

You might want to make your front door a permanent boundary. If so, just walk out it one day, and if your dog follows you across, go into a correction mode. You want to behave just as you did when you worked on the Stay Back command, only of course here you will not be using any command, just your correction.

Or you may have your own gate that, for safety reasons, you'd like to know your dog would not pass through, even if it were left open. If that's the situation, establish that gate as a permanent boundary and work on it. Have the gate open and move around in front of it while your dog is behind it. Or pass back and forth through it and make it clear with your corrections that your dog knows he can't follow after you. The better he understands the boundary the more you should increase distractions that might tempt him. In this way you can build his respect for the limitation of the boundary.

Property Lines

I've also set up my property line as a permanent boundary. For one thing I would hate to see my dog get hit by a car; for another, I figure if my neighbor wanted a dog he'd get one. You might have a place on your property where you'd like your dog to stop and go no further. It could be the edge of your lawn, or the sidewalk, or it could be a corner designated by a point like a tree or shrub. Wherever the line is, start enforcing it as a permanent boundary by crossing the line while you keep an eye on your dog. As soon as you see him cross it, correct him. Run him back, and make it clear to him how far he can go. Just as when you taught him the Stay Back command, cross over to his side of the line and give him a pat. Let him know that he's free to move around, or follow after you, on the correct side of the line. Then turn around and cross the perimeter line a few feet from the spot where you originally crossed. Repeat this process of crossing and re-crossing for the entire length of the line you've designated a permanent boundary. Correct your dog whenever he crosses the line, wherever he crosses it. Once you establish these boundaries be sure that in the beginning you test your dog with them frequently.

You should be aware, though, that establishing permanent boundaries around the perimeter of your property with this method of training is not foolproof. It's not intended as a means for you to set up these boundaries and then leave your dog behind them for the day. If you live in an area where a fence is not feasible, and you want to be assured that your dog will not cross your boundary, go to www.dogwatch.com. Here you can locate a nearby dealer who can set up the best hidden fence system on the market for you.

When Can Your Dog Cross a Permanent Boundary?

Your dog cannot cross a permanent boundary unless you give him the Break command, or the Come command, or even a Heel command. However there is one exception to this rule. If you have your dog on a leash he must follow and stay within the six-foot range of that leash. In that case you don't have to command him to come with you; he must.

The Safety Factor

Don't underestimate your dog's intelligence. He can learn permanent boundaries, and teaching him these could save his life. I had one client who had just started training when she got out of her car in a department store parking lot, couldn't stop her dog from jumping out after her, and saw her dog get run over and killed. Another client who hadn't yet learned to establish permanent boundaries left a gate open and also lost her dog to an accident with a passing car.

I did have a client, though, who pulled into a parking lot, saw a vehicle start to roll down a slope toward her, and bailed out, leaving the car door open behind her. Because we had worked on boundaries, her dog stayed in the car in this emergency situation and wasn't hurt.

Remember: once you have established your boundaries, be sure to test your dog on them. Get out of your car and start running away. Watch to see if your dog will make a mistake. Be sure to be consistent and build your dog's ability to acknowledge permanent boundaries. In this way you'll have covered your bases in case of an emergency.

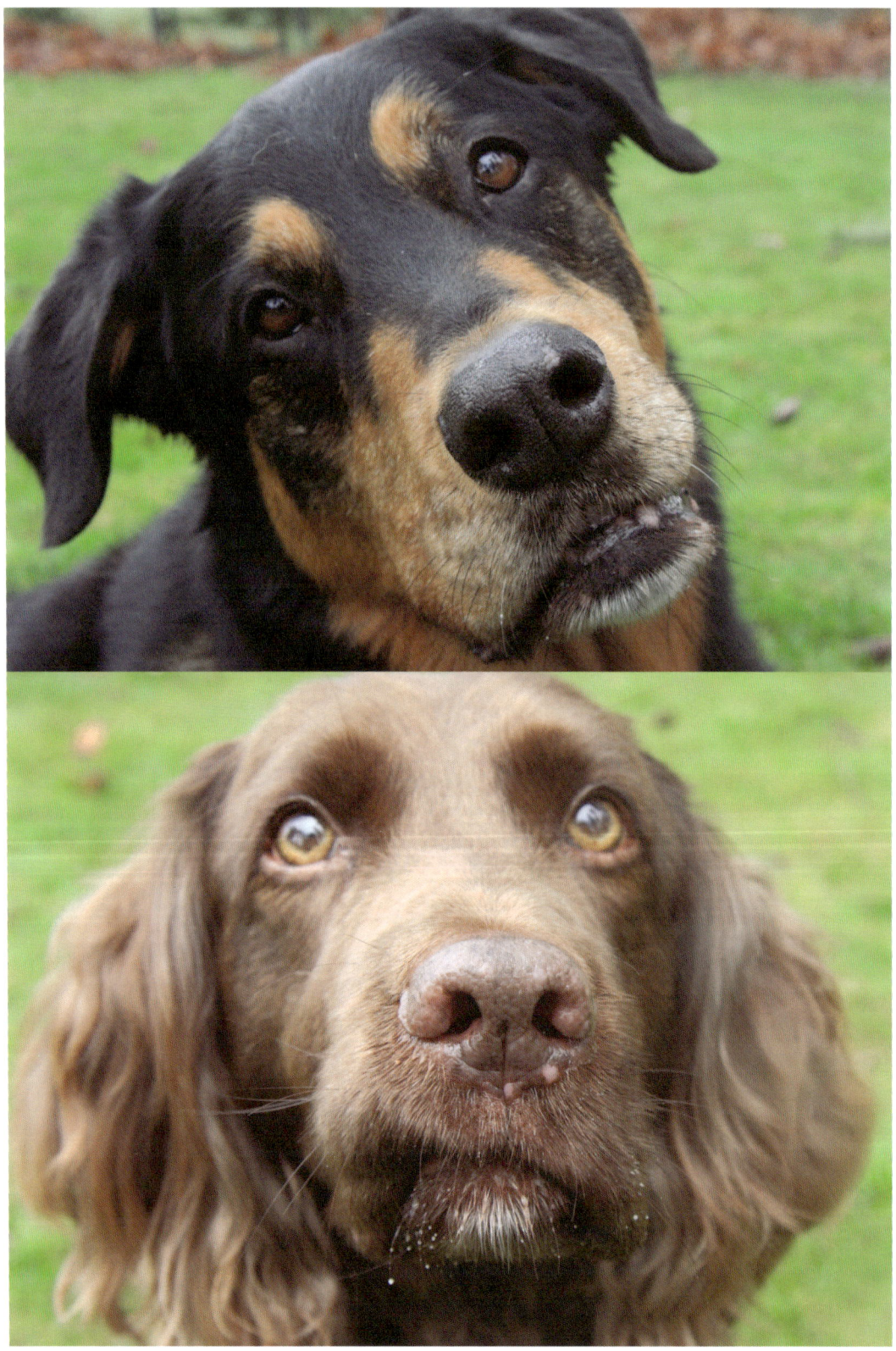

Simon and Tawney.

[CHAPTER 18]

Resisting the Distraction of Another Dog

IN THE LAST LESSON OF THE OBEDIENCE SERIES WE provide a distraction for the client and his dog, and this is something you should be ready to try yourself. At this point you and your dog should know Heeling, Staying, Break, Come, the Finish, and Down and Sit from the side and from the front. Now you need to see if you can do these things with another dog right next to your own.

The Other Dog: A Permanent Don't Touch

We use a well-trained dog for this procedure to make it easier for the client and his dog. If that isn't available to you, you should find a helper who can at least walk in a Patrol position with his dog.

The other dog is going to be a permanent Don't Touch for your dog, which means if your dog makes any attempt to make contact he will get a correction. You want to take away his intention to make contact with any dog, unless the dogs are introduced on your terms.

Encountering the Other Dog

For this procedure to be most effective, the initial positioning of the dogs is very important. You should be behind a wall or some other screen, and have your dog in the Heel position. You want the sight of the other dog to be a surprise to your dog, so the helper and his dog should walk forward from the other side of the wall, come out maybe ten feet ahead of your dog, and continue forward. Just as the other dog appears, give your dog a Heel command and follow after them.

With your dog on a Heel, follow the other dog.

Drop the slack of your leash and create the "brick wall" effect.

Get your dog to turn from the other dog.

As you head toward the rear of your helper's dog, watch your dog closely to see if he will take the bait and forge ahead, trying to make contact with the other dog's hind end. Be ready to react if you see your dog move forward suddenly. Drop the two feet of slack you have in your hand as you make a sharp Right-About Turn, and try to do this without your dog seeing you do it. If you drop your line and move quickly, it will be as if your dog gets the "brick wall effect," causing a very effective correction just before he makes contact with the other dog. Immediately after this maneuver, pick up your slack, and you should be back in the Heel position.

Pick up your slack.

Watch to see if your dog looks back.

Keep walking and watch for your dog to try to turn around and look back. If he does, speed up and make a quick leash correction. Remember, you told him to Heel, and he's supposed to be watching *you,* not another dog. Your job at this point is to use the maneuvers and corrections you learned in the Heeling lessons to get—and keep—his attention on you, regardless of the distraction the other dog may present.

Repeat the procedure by having your helper turn and come toward you, then turn around again. You should also turn so that once again the rear of his dog is in front of your dog. If you made your initial Right–About correction effectively, your dog should be watching you as he Heels, instead of trying to forge ahead and make contact with the other dog. Continue this process. Follow the other dog for a while and keep making Right–About Turns until your dog is making the turns with you without needing a correction. Don't forget to praise him if he's keeping himself in the correct position.

The Pass By

The next step is to have your dog on a Break and have your helper's dog pass by on a Patrol or Heel. You want the other dog to be close enough so that your dog has the opportunity to reach out and make contact with it. Remember the other dog is what we call a permanent Don't Touch. It's all right for your dog to look at him—he just can't lean or step toward him. If your dog does try to make contact, step back and make a sharp correction with your Leash. This correction should be the same one you made when you worked on Don't Touch with the food temptation in Chapter 13.

Have your helper make passes by until your dog turns away as he sees them approach. Now you're teaching your dog to ignore other dogs. Your dog should not make an attempt to make contact with any other dogs unless you bring him up and introduce them on your terms.

If at any point in this exercise your dog moves aggressively after your helper's dog, give

Have helper walk by when your dog is on Break.

an "Out!" command and choke up on the collar as you use your leash to give your dog a severe shake side to side. Do this in a dominating fashion and make it clear that this aggression will not be tolerated.

Side by Side

On a Heel

Walk with your dog on a Heel and have the other dog pass at your side, heading in the other direction. As the dogs pass each other, watch carefully to see if your dog will try to make contact. If he does, correct him by making a sharp side step.

Make a sharp side step if your dog tries to make contact.

Turn around and pass side by side again. Do this until your dog shows no interest in the other dog as it goes by him.

On a Sit–Stay

If your helper has the control to do this next exercise, leave both the dogs on a Sit–Stay side by side. Practice telling each dog to Down and Sit. Be ready to step in and correct if your dog shows any interest in the other one, or if your dog responds to the other handler's commands.

Leave the dogs on a Sit–Stay side by side.

Responding to "Break"

Have your helper give his dog a Break command and see if your dog responds. You could also have the helper call his dog with "Come."

If your dog Breaks or Comes on the helper's command, you must correct him—place him back in the Stay position—and teach him to wait for *your* command only.

When both dogs are on Break, remember that the same permanent Don't Touch rule still applies.

In group class, all other dogs are a permanent "Don't Touch."

If you were at our training center, the next step would be to place you and your dog in a group class with twenty other people who have been through the same training program. In this case your dog would be on a permanent Don't Touch with all other dogs in the class.

Part 3

Questions and Answers

Instead of just training my dog to do things, you are training me how to get past the frustration of disobedience without hitting or yelling. I thought you had to force a dog to do what you wanted, yet watching how easily you get a dog to want to do what you tell him changed my attitude.

—C. Gilcrease

I had taken my dog Maggie to training elsewhere for a month, and she could only sit and mildly obey walking on a leash. You may pay more for Ron Pace's Training program, but in one month's time you'll learn more than you would in six months of training elsewhere. Maggie has stopped jumping the fence, digging up our yard, and comes when you call her. She is truly a different dog than she was just one month ago. [For this training] you will not regret the time involved. This is of value that goes beyond money. You've acquired a skill!

— W. Chittenden

1. If my spouse does the training, will the dog work for me?

I often get asked the question, "If one member of the family trains the dog, will the dog obey other family members?" And my answer is, "Maybe. Maybe not."

One factor in this area is the type of dog involved. For instance, my brother-in-law has a golden retriever that has such a strong desire to please that if practically *anyone* picked up his leash and gave him a command, he would be more than willing to obey. At the other extreme are most dogs I see, who aren't eager to work for the person doing the training, let alone anyone else. Some of these dogs force their owners to learn exactly how to make them work, or they won't work for them at all.

You might look at it like this—some dogs are less intelligent and will just go along with you. Others are smart and will always try to outsmart you. Having intelligence doesn't necessarily make a dog easier to train. If you want a dog that will be easier to train, look for one that wants to please you.

The bond you have with your dog will also make a difference. The relationship you have with him, especially if you've raised him from puppyhood; the amount of time you've spent with him; and whether he's been raised indoors or outdoors will all make a difference in ease of training.

So when I'm asked the question about who the dog will work for, I usually respond by asking the questioner if he has a computer. If he does I tell him that I'm sure he knows a computer can do a lot if a person knows how to use it. It's the same thing where his dog is concerned. Some people will be able to make the dog respond better than others will.

Your dog will work best for whoever *knows how* to work him best.

> *The most common problem in getting a dog to respond to anyone is this: once your dog knows you, or someone else, will not back up a command, he knows you didn't mean it and the command doesn't need to be obeyed.*

2. How do I stop my dog's digging?

If you've skipped through this book just to find a solution for digging, you'll probably be wasting your time. You need to build a foundation of communication between you and your dog before you can effectively solve this—or any other—problem. For instance, I want to be sure my dog knows the Don't Touch command before I start correcting him for digging, since I know if he understands that command he knows how to turn away from things.

So assuming you've laid the necessary foundation for communication with your dog, let's get into correcting him for what many consider very undesirable behavior. Especially if a well-landscaped yard is involved.

When it comes to the issue of digging, I believe one of the most common mistakes people make is to let their emotions get the best of them. Some people get very emotionally wrapped up in their yard after spending hours of effort and/or money on it. When they come home from a hard day's work and see that their bored dog, who has been waiting for them all day, couldn't find anything

better to do than dig a nice big hole in the middle of their lawn, they become extremely upset. Along with disappointment in the dog comes anger, and anger can be one of your worse enemies in communicating to your dog what you do and don't want him to do.

If you step out your door, see some damage, and become very angry, your dog will know it. While you're yelling "Why did you do that?" he may slink down or cower. By his body language you might think he knew what he did wrong, but that wouldn't be true. Instead he'd be totally focused on your anger and not on whatever you were trying to show or tell him. At that point, I'd suggest you give him a pat on the back, go into the house, pour yourself a glass of wine, and relax.

When you are relaxed, put your leash on your dog, go into your back yard, and give your dog an obedience workout. Finish him, Heel with him, Down him, Sit him, call him, leave him on a Stay, and so forth. Make sure you maintain a neutral attitude, not expressing any anger over the hole, as you work with him.

After you've worked with him for a few minutes, walk with him on Break over to the hole he dug. Bend down over the hole with your legs spread apart and start digging, flipping the dirt out behind you. Let your dog see what you're doing and look to see his reaction. After he's watched you flipping the dirt out, bring him close, grasp his collar at the back of his neck with both hands, and hold his head down in the hole.

You don't need to hold his nose in the dirt; having his head a few inches from the ground is fine. Hold him there for five to ten seconds without saying a word or displaying any anger.

Next slide your hands up the leash and give a couple of quick snaps away from the hole.

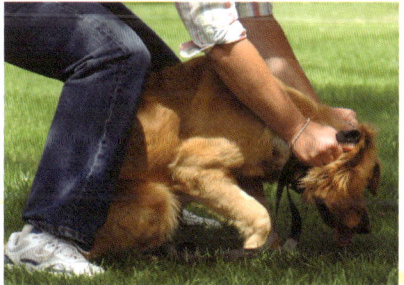
Hold your dog's head down toward the hole.

Give a couple of snaps away.

You want to snap your dog away just as you would if you were making a Don't Touch correction on the hole. As shown in the photographs, you want to be sure to release your dog as soon as you've made the correction.

Release your dog right after the correction.

Resume walking.

Resume walking on Break with your dog. Slowly walk over to the hole again and repeat your digging action. Hold his head down to the hole just as you did before and follow with your Don't Touch correction away from the hole. Repeat this sequence several times until you see your dog move to the end of his leash and show he'd prefer to stay away when he sees you start to dig. When you reach that point, verbally praise him for wanting nothing to do with the hole.

By going through this process you're showing your dog that digging causes corrective actions. You want him to associate digging with his own discomfort so that when he sees the dirt being flipped, it indicates behavior he wants to avoid.

If I were planting something and my dog came over to investigate, I would pull him into the hole and correct him away from it. If you think your dog can't understand what you're trying to tell him with your actions, you're mistaken. Why do you think he might pull up plants you planted the day before? Because he watched you plant them.

Over the years I've tried many methods to stop dogs from digging, and I believe this method is the best by far, as long as it's used consistently. It is not a one-time correction. After you've gone through this procedure you can fill in the holes your dog dug, take him out the next day, and correct him again. Even if he hasn't dug a hole one day you can take him out on-leash, dig your own hole, and correct him away from it. If you do this on a regular basis you'll see that your dog will want nothing to do with anything that resembles digging.

As with any other aspect of training, conditioning is very important if you want to stop unwanted behavior. If you take your dog to the beach and he wants to dig in the sand, you must correct him there, just as you would if he were in your back yard. The more he digs when you can't or don't choose to correct him, the longer it will take for you to make him stop.

3. How can I make my dog stop chewing my things?

Just as I mentioned in dealing with digging, if you're concerned that your dog is chewing on things—from your couch or your shoes to the siding on your house—you must first lay a *foundation of obedience training* and teach your dog the Don't Touch command before you can tackle this problem.

Remember the two types of Don't Touch—temporary and permanent? If you never want your dog to touch your shoes in the first place, they would be a permanent Don't Touch. That means anytime you see him attempt to grab a shoe, or anything else he's never to take, you must drop whatever you happen to be doing at that time and go for him.

If you time your response correctly, your dog should know what he did to trigger your attention. If he hears you and pulls away before you can reach him, you must go after him and take him back to the shoe, or whatever the item was, so you can correct him away from it. By using his leash, his tab, or even the end of his chain, make two quick snaps away to turn him in the other direction. Have his Nylabone handy to throw down for him so he can see what he *can* have, as well as what he can't.

If you come home and find that your dog has chewed on the carpet or the furniture in your absence, take a tip from the section on digging. Before you do anything else, *calm down*. When you are calm, you should put your leash on your dog and take him outside for an obedience lesson. After working him for a while, walk him on Break up to the area where he chewed and pick up and put back pieces of carpeting, or upholstery, one at time. As you replace the piece of carpeting, pull him up to it and correct him away from it, recreating his mistake and correcting him as you would for a permanent Don't Touch.

Repeat this process without saying a word and without showing any anger toward your dog.

Just as you demonstrated digging to show your dog what to avoid, you could also pull back at the item he chewed as if you were ripping it away yourself. By doing this you could try to recreate his earlier tearing actions and then make your correction.

Later in the day you may want to have a helper take the chewed item—the shoe, the piece of carpet—and approach your dog with it. Remember using food to tempt your dog when you taught him a temporary Don't Touch? Treat the chewed item the same way you did the food in that case and make your correction if your dog shows any interest in it. Your dog should automatically turn away from the object when he's approached.

Throw his Nylabone down, use your "Take It" command, and praise him when he goes for it. Once again, you would show him what he can have, not just what he can't. And remember: this is not a one-time correction. You must be consistent with your corrections if you want to eliminate this behavior.

4. How can I create an outdoor area for my dog?

If you have the space, one of the smartest investments you can make for yourself and your dog is an outdoor kennel, or a fenced area intended solely for him. Not to be confused with a crate, which is an excellent tool for housebreaking, a kennel is more what you might consider a dog run, or an area for your dog to "hang out." Along with a fenced yard, it's one of the things I think you should have if you're going to own a dog. I call the kennel a "babysitter." If you're gone for long periods of time and can't watch your dog properly, or if you want him out of the way when you have visitors, this is a safe place to put him. It could also save you money from destructiveness—

An example of a kennel.

either in your home or outdoors. In fact, you should be very careful about letting your dog have the run of your yard unsupervised for long periods of time.

You can make your kennel both dog-friendly and dog-safe. The standard size is about seven feet by fourteen feet. Some fence companies will build one for you or provide a ready-made version. You may even be able to find these online. They can come in a number of different sizes and configurations, and you can determine what is best for your situation. If you plan to build your own I would recommend using a minimum of 11-gauge cyclone fence material. Nine-gauge is even better, and you should know that a dog can destroy 13-gauge wire in a heartbeat.

While you certainly could—and it may help for sanitary reasons—you don't need to place the kennel on a concrete slab. An alternative surface would be galvanized wire-like fencing attached to the bottom of the kennel with about four or five inches of pea gravel placed on top. If your dog attempts to dig in the gravel he will hit the wire, and this will help deter him from digging in other situations.

You should also plan on covering at least half of the kennel with a roof. This could be made of a waterproof or water-resistant material. Fence companies make metal bars that clamp on top of your kennel so that you can strap material over it for a roof.

You also can put a doghouse inside your kennel or, better yet, have the kennel built with a small doorway so that you can put a doghouse on the outside of the kennel and provide your dog with more kennel space.

One of the most common problems people have when they put their dog in a kennel is barking. Actually the kennel is an excellent place to teach your dog to stop barking. See the next question for more on this topic.

5. How do I stop my dog's barking?

There are many different reasons why a dog barks. He may be trying to alert you that someone is coming, he may want to go outside or come inside, he may respond to a neighbor dog's barking, or he may be bored, or excited, or want to play ball, or go for a walk, or maybe he just wants to protest your training. For instance, you may tell him to Sit and Stay, and he may bark back at you.

There are times to bark and times not to bark, and realizing this is your first step in curbing barking. I like to teach my dog how to stop barking on command. In this way I am determining when it's appropriate or all right for him to bark, and stopping him when the barking is not acceptable.

I would start teaching this lesson when my dog is young, and the best place to do it is in his kennel. If you put your dog inside his kennel, at some point—it may even be right away—he will start barking. He wants you to come over and let him out. When this happens, let him get into a barking spell for a few minutes, and position yourself around the corner, hopefully out of sight, with a garden hose nozzle in hand. When you are ready, step around the corner and give a deep-toned "Out!" command. You can use a different command, such as "Quiet!" but the "Out!" command is a dominating

noise that mimics the sound of a mother dog warning her pups. That is the warning command I use. After you give your warning, step back so that you are out of sight.

Now wait for the next bark. As soon as your dog barks, step forward, give the "Out!" command, and simultaneously deliver a quick shot of water to his face.

Once you've sprayed him, step back again and wait for the next bark. Be ready to repeat your actions as soon as you hear it. Timing and consistency are very critical here. Once your dog knows that his bark will trigger the spray of water, he'll quiet down.

I had to deal with this issue concerning a five-month-old Lab the other day. It took three shots of water, a follow-up half an hour later, and the Out command was learned. It may take you ten or twelve shots the first time you try this approach, but don't stop until your dog is quiet.

If your dog stays quiet for a few minutes, you could go up to the kennel and praise him, but be ready to act when you turn your back and walk away. That's just when he might try another bark. If he does, spin around, give your "Out!" command as you run for the hose, and give him a shot of water. Don't let your dog get away with even one bark. You don't want him to think that you'll only correct him sometimes. If your dog sees you coming and runs into his dog house, deliver the spray of water anyway. If you don't, it would be as if your dog crossed a boundary, or touched a Don't Touch item and then backed off as soon as he saw you. You don't want to let him get away with disobedience. If you want him to comply with your commands, he must receive a correction.

It's also important that your dog know you can deter his barking without the garden hose. For instance, if you're training him and he barks when you leave him on a Stay, or because he's distracted by movement elsewhere, correct him in this way: move his choke chain up until it's just beneath his ears, and give your "Out!" command when he starts to bark. If you've done your job well enough with the garden hose he may stop at your command, but if he decides to test you, be ready to intensify your correction. Move your hand to a point on the leash about six inches from the clip and give a couple of quick snaps on your dog's collar.

Even if you haven't worked on the hose technique and introduced the "Out" command previously, repeat your command now. If your dog doesn't respond to the quick snaps, you may need to go from giving him a snap with the leash to giving him a good shake.

When you're making this correction be aware of your timing. You must catch your dog with a correction just as the noise is starting to come from his mouth. And you mustn't stop your correction until he stops barking.

However, be sure that you don't start this correction process if you see that your dog is barking for a very strong reason, such as someone walking toward you with another dog. Initially, start teaching your dog to stop barking at your command in situations where you believe the corrections should be minimal, then work your way into more challenging situations. If you feel that a distraction is too hard for your dog to resist, you could also make a couple of corrections and then walk him away from the situation. In this way you could avoid getting too heavily into correcting him.

You might also face a situation where your dog obeys you but needs to be corrected again and again. I had one client with a German shepherd that would start barking in the middle of the night for no apparent reason. She would yell "Out!" and her dog would be silent for a few hours then start barking again. In this instance I told her to stop giving him the command. Instead she was to jump out of bed at the first barking sound and use her tab to give her dog a good shake correction.

If your dog is barking for a good reason—say, to alert you that someone is approaching your house—praise him. If he's barking when he shouldn't be, correct him with an automatic correction. This will teach your dog when he can bark and when he can't.

When someone comes to your door it's a slightly different situation. If you want your dog to let you know someone has come to the door, but you want him quiet after sounding the alarm, praise him for letting you know someone is there and then give him the "Out" command. It's as if you were saying, "Thanks for letting me know, now that's enough."

6. What if my dog barks in the car when I'm driving?

Barking in the car is another problem. I've had a lot of clients who drive with dogs that bark at other animals, cars, or motorcycles. If you have this situation, put a prong collar on your dog, attach your leash to the collar, and hold the leash loop in your thumb as you drive. If you drive a large vehicle like an SUV, you can clip or tie two leashes together so that the leash length can reach you. Your leverage isn't very good in correcting at this angle, so the prong collar will give you better results than your dog's choke chain would.

As soon as your dog starts to bark, be ready to make a correction. If your dog has already learned the "Out" command for barking, he should know what it means to be corrected for something he shouldn't be doing. Be ready to make an automatic correction by giving him a sharp snap with your leash as soon as he starts to bark. Don't give him a command; just give him a correction. Remember: you don't want to give him a command to stop barking at things he never should have been barking at in the first place.

7. Does it matter if I let my dog get up on the bed?

I believe that most dogs should not be on their masters' beds because of the issue of dominance. In your relationship with your dog, it's important that you be the pack leader. Allowing your dog on the bed can make him think that instead of being subservient to you, he's of equal status.

But even though I don't recommend that you allow your dog on the furniture, I realize that there are people who enjoy their dogs' company on the bed. If you are one of these people, you should be prepared for the possible consequences of your decision to permit this behavior.

Some dogs may actually get so comfortable and proprietary on the bed that when a family member tries to move them they give a growl, as if to say, "Leave me alone." If this happens to you, you

really have a problem—and it's not a problem you want to have. This is why, unless you want to take the chance of jeopardizing your relationship with your dog, my advice is that you keep him off the bed.

That being said, there are some things you can do that will help if you do decide you want to permit your dog to be on the bed. To begin with, don't allow him on unless you call him up first. And if you want him to get off, call him off and correct him with a tug if he doesn't move at your command. This approach can be used where other furniture is concerned as well.

8. How do I keep my dog off the furniture?

You should treat your furniture as a permanent boundary, and you should correct your dog as you would if he crossed any permanent boundary. To correct your dog for jumping on your furniture, start your correction the moment he steps on the item you want him to avoid. Let him hear you coming. Charge after him, grab his tab or collar, and drag him off the bed or sofa. As he falls from the furniture you're finished with the correction, so turn it off.

Grab his collar or tab.

Don't keep staring at him—which would make him feel there is still something wrong even though he may be off the furniture. Remember that your correction is over until he steps back up there again.

If your dog gets on the bed or couch, sees you coming, and then jumps off, you must pull him back up on the bed so that you can pull him off. You want to recreate his mistake so that you can still correct him for it even if he's moved.

Turn off your correction as soon as he's off the chair.

The same rule applies if you should come home and see a wrinkled bedspread or hair on the sofa, and know that your dog has been on the furniture in your absence. In this case you should take him back up where he was and correct him off.

> *It's worth mentioning that in making such a correction you should not let your emotions get away from you so that you show your dog you are frustrated, exasperated, or angry. Do not sigh, yell, or in other ways show your displeasure. Simply make your correction dispassionately. In this way the dog's attention will be focused on the correction for his behavior—not on your mood.*

9. What if my dog jumps on doors?

Before you try to correct this problem—or any other problem, for that matter—you must first build a foundation for communication with your dog by teaching him the training lessons described this book. With regard to this specific problem, your dog must understand boundaries and Don't Touch.

Remember the beginning of your training, when you learned to correct your dog for jumping on you and others? You used your leash to make effective corrections, fine-tuning the angle of the correction, and you became conscious of timing—when to start the correction and when to finish it. You also learned that when you decide to make a correction, you should not stop correcting until your dog stops the undesirable behavior. All these elements are important in dealing with the "jumping on doors" issue.

As soon as your dog's feet hit the door, you should let him know that this behavior triggered a response from you. Stomp your feet or make other noises to let him know that you're coming after him. If he's outside and you're inside, open the door and go after him. (See the lesson on off-leash Come and the chase game to stop him from running from you). Grab his tab, run him back to the door, and when you reach it, quickly pull him up to the place on the door where he had his paws.

In this way you're recreating his mistake. Then make an abrupt snap at a downward angle and release your tab when he's in mid-air. Go back into the house and wait for him to jump on the door again so that you can repeat the process.

Make sure that you start your correction—going after him—just when his paws hit the door. You can't be lazy about this and get up slowly. You must jump up as soon as your dog's feet hit the door. Finish your correction when you release his tab. Don't say anything or look at him after you release him, because you've finished correcting him at that point.

For this process to be effective, you should never allow your dog to jump on the door without receiving a correction. This is conditioning. If you think he might jump on the door when you're not there to correct him, put him in his kennel. Only let him have the run of the yard when you're available to make the proper corrections. Remember: for your corrections to be effective and create a change in behavior, your dog cannot be corrected when you're there and then discover that when you're not there he won't be corrected. Set him up. Make him think you're not at home sometime. Have someone start your car and leave while you wait quietly for an opportunity to catch your dog "in the act" so that you can correct him.

Once you've made some consistent corrections and it looks as though your dog has gotten the message, go outside and praise him. After that he should began to realize that if he tries to jump on the door again, the attention he'll get from jumping will be negative. Attention he'll receive for not jumping will be positive.

Some dogs may paw at the door instead of jumping on it. To correct that behavior just pull your dog straight into the door and then give a quick snap back—about six to eight inches from the door. Use your common sense here—what you want to do is recreate your dog's mistake as best as you can

so that you can make the proper correction for that mistake. Remember he should never get away with jumping or pawing at the door again.

If your dog jumps up on the door, hears you coming to correct him, and then gets to avoid the correction by running from you, you would be teaching him that all he has to do to avoid a correction is jump and run. You *must* correct your dog every time he makes this mistake.

This rule also applies to jumping on people or countertops—or anywhere he shouldn't be jumping, but does, and then backs off before you can reach him. You must go after your dog, get him, bring him back to the scene of the mistake, pull him up to recreate the mistake, and then snap him down. Remember to release him in mid-air and turn away at that point. Don't stand there looking at your dog after you finish the correction. You don't want him to think that he's still being corrected, and you don't want him to think that he has to sit and wait. Your correction should have released him into a Break, not into a Sit position.

10. What if I want my dog to play with another dog?

Remember: never let your dog initiate contact with any other dog. If you *want* him to make contact with another dog, take your dog up to the other and use a command like "Make Friends." Make it clear to your dog that you are the one deciding when this will happen.

11. What if we're approached by an unknown dog?

Working with your dog in a training field is one thing. There you are around dogs handled by owners who have spent time and effort to teach obedience to their dogs. But being in other environments, where there may be stray dogs or owners who do not respect your space, is another thing altogether.

I had one client who had an English mastiff she showed in conformation matches. Her dog had always been well adjusted with other dogs around him until the day a dachshund happened to bite his hind leg while his back was turned. The client came to me because she couldn't show her dog any more after that happened. After the bite, her mastiff was always on the defensive, ready to go after any dog that came near him. We corrected this problem by not only taking away the dog's intention to defend himself, but by teaching the handler how to protect her dog. We wanted the dog to feel that he didn't have to take care of this problem himself. If he could have confidence in his handler to protect him from other dogs, he could relax.

This issue—being approached by other dogs—has been and always will be a problem for responsible dog owners who would like to walk their dog down the street without being confronted by leashed and unleashed dogs. For some reason, many people seem to think that just because two dogs are passing, they should be able to stop and sniff, or otherwise make contact with one another. Aside from the problem that not all dogs are approachable, not all owners may want to have someone else deciding if their dog should make contact with another.

Often, if you happen to object, the person walking toward you will say something like, "Oh, don't worry, my dog is friendly." You can discourage them by saying, "Well, mine is not." And if you find yourself in tight quarters, go to the Patrol position—*you* be the one in control of your dog.

If an unleashed dog comes after you, you need to determine how big a threat this dog is to you and your dog. If it's a happy-go-lucky Lab or golden retriever, you might decide it's all right to let the dogs meet. In any case, you make the call whether to allow contact or to just keep walking ahead with your dog in the Patrol position.

Prevent unknown dogs from making contact with your dog.

If you choose to keep walking ahead, usually the other dog will try to come up behind your dog to get an air scent of him. If the dog comes too close you can spin around to your right and give a loud yell. If I do this just before they are able to make contact with my dog, it usually sends them running.

If you have a real threat on your hands, you'll want to have some backup. I tell my clients to decide for themselves how they want to protect themselves from a dog attack. Whether you carry a cane, a baseball bat, a loud whistle, pepper spray, or even a firearm, in most places in the country you do have the right to protect yourself and your dog from being attacked.

12. What do you think about electronic collars?

Many people think an electronic collar will virtually train their dog for them at the touch of a button. I wish it were that simple. Electronic collars do have their place as a tool and an aid in obedience training and problem solving; the dilemma is that you must know how to use one properly or you will do more harm than good.

Fortunately new technology has made these tools far better than they once were. Older collars usually had one setting from the transmitter (the control in your hand). This meant that when you hit the button to deliver the stimulation, the dog would get too much stimulation and be "overcorrected." If too high a setting is used, a dog can go into a panic and not be able to think about why he is receiving a shock. With the new digital systems, the level of correction can be finely controlled with a dial on the transmitter. You can actually start at zero and dial up bit, by bit to the point where your dog just feels as if he has an itch he wants to scratch. Factoring in your dog's coat and his pain tolerance, you can set your control just high enough that he will feel as if he's received a snap on his collar when you want to correct him.

Ideally the use of an electronic collar should be explained by an experienced trainer. What follows is an example of a way I have used an electric collar:

I had a client who had a large Shiloh shepherd that was way too much dog for her. She went through our obedience program and was doing fine until one day when she was taking her dog for a walk and a loose dog charged and attacked her dog. After that her shepherd was on the defensive, always looking for a threat and ready to be the aggressor toward any dog in sight. This problem completely destroyed my client's enjoyment of walking her dog through the neighborhood.

In using an electric collar to solve this problem, I first instructed my client to put the collar on her dog during the day and take it off at night for a week. I wanted the dog to get used to the collar so she wouldn't suspect it as the cause when she received a correction from it. It's also good if you associate something positive with the act when you put the collar on your dog—for instance, put it on and then feed your dog. Put it on and play ball. Put it on and go for a walk.

After her dog had been wearing the collar for a week, I had my client take her for a walk while I followed, watching them from my car. One of the reasons I kept myself out of sight was because I wanted the dog to think the correction was coming entirely from her owner. I told my client to walk in a Patrol position and give a quick leash correction when her dog started to lunge and show aggression. At the same time that happened I would apply just the right amount of stimulation from the transmitter in my hand. When these actions occurred simultaneously, I could see that her dog was surprised she was able to make such an effective correction.

The next dog we came across elicited the same aggressive response from the shepherd. My client did the same thing—made a quick leash correction—and I made sure that again her dog received the stimulation. When we encountered a third dog I bumped the level up a little, and her dog must have finally associated the correction with undesirable behavior, because by the time we got to the fourth and fifth dog the behavior stopped entirely. With every dog they encountered after that, the shepherd walked very nicely for her owner without displaying any outburst of aggression. In this case the proper use of an electronic collar allowed this owner to continue one of her most favorite activities: taking her dog out for walks. Some may criticize using an electronic collar on dogs in any situation, without ever realizing what a valuable tool it can be in the right hands.

13. What do I do when my dog tries to snatch food from my child?

Food in others' hands, including a child's, should be a permanent Don't Touch and you should correct your dog accordingly. See Chapter 13.

14. How do I handle my dog when guests come to the door?

Before you open the door, put your leash on your dog and see if he is going to bark. Let him have the chance to sound an alarm, and then command him to stop. If he doesn't stop, be ready to follow through with the proper correction (see the answer to "How do I stop my dog's barking?"). When your guests enter your home, prepare to automatically correct any jumping. Once your rules in these areas have been enforced and you have control over the barking and jumping, the next step is to decide if you want your dog to make some contact with the visitors or none at all.

Give your dog the Don't Touch command when you are ready.

Remember: when people come into his territory you should give him a Don't Touch command. This is an exception to the "people as a permanent Don't Touch rule." If you do want him to make contact with the visitors you can then bring him up to them and tell him, "Make Friends."

If you don't want him to have any contact with them you could also take your dog to another room or some other place where he can see what's going on and give him a Stay Back command. In this way he can observe you and your guests without being in the same area.

15. My dog begs for food at the table. How do I stop it?

It's my belief that you should never give your dog any food other than what you normally feed him every day. If you feed him different types of food I think he will always wait for something better. Find the best dog food available and stay with it; then your dog won't be looking for other handouts.

If he is interested in begging for any food, make the object of his attention a permanent Don't Touch and correct him accordingly.

16. How do I stop my dog from chasing my cat?

If you have a cat that lives with you and your dog, you have to have some rules. The first rule I would make is that the dog and cat can make contact with each other, but neither can agitate or tease the other.

Timing and consistency will be the way you show your dog what he can and cannot do with the cat. Like a referee in a boxing match, your job will be to step in at the right moment and stop your dog from crossing the cut-off line. If you see your dog stalking, chasing, or behaving too aggressively toward the cat, that behavior should be your cut-off point. When your dog goes to chase the cat, you're going to chase the dog.

To correct his behavior, grab him by the tab and back him off away from the cat just as you did with a Don't Touch. The difference here is that your dog does not have to stay away from the cat; he just can't chase the cat. So don't turn him completely away, just back him off a little.

If you have a big bully dog that is way too dominate over the cat, prepare yourself with a throw chain when you think he may go for the cat. Give an under-handed toss at his hind end at the beginning of his cat chase and go after him just as you would if he were running from your Come command.

17. How do I introduce my dog to a second dog I've adopted?

A good way to bring a new dog into your household is to first start by choosing a dog of the opposite sex. Your best prescription for success will be to have dogs of opposite sexes—not to have two kings or two queens in one castle.

If your dog and the new dog are older, say a year old or more, take them for a walk on neutral ground. By neutral I mean not in your dog's territory. Have both dogs leashed, with separate handlers, and walk them about twenty-plus feet apart. As you follow each other, periodically change direction so that the dog that was behind becomes the dog in front. In this way you allow the dog following to get the scent of the dog leading, and each can determine that the other is no threat. Shorten the distance between you every time you change direction.

After turning or changing direction several times, and gradually moving in closer and closer, walk side by side with the dogs in a Patrol position. Be sure you're always keeping them under control. As they start to feel comfortable around each other, you can try giving each a loose leash and allowing them to make contact on a Break. Remember to try to keep the leashes loose so you don't create any tension or friction between them.

If you see one become aggressive over the other, you can give a hard snap back and break it up. Then resume walking side by side for a while longer to see if they can get along again. You will know the dogs enough to know if one is a fighter or not. If everything seems to be going okay at this point, you might try turning them loose in a fenced yard and observe from a distance.

18. Can I teach my dog to stand still?

Sometimes this command is referred to as Stand for Examination. Being able to have your dog stand and not move from his position is something you may find very useful. It helps if you're trying to wipe wet paws or groom your dog. I usually trim my dog's toenails while he's lying down, but it's also handy to be able to do it while he's standing. And of course it's helpful to have him stand when you or your veterinarian examines him. I teach this command along with a hand signal (see photo) from the Heel position.

As I give the verbal command "Stand," and make a forward-motion signal with my right hand, I make a light tug on the dog's collar with the leash—again using my right hand. This tug must be made in a straight, forward movement since I want to get the dog to rise from his

Give a hand signal as you say, "Stand."

sitting position. The angle of your tug has to be level—straight forward or slightly lower forward. (Remember if you tug forward and upward, you'll place your dog in a Sit).

As the dog starts to stand, I bring my left hand down and use the lightest amount of contact to stroke his right side. I do this with a slow movement, continuing the stroke toward his flank. I want the touch to be so slow and soothing that he doesn't want to move. On a first attempt I Break him just as my hand starts to leave his side and before he moves. Then I repeat this procedure over and over, being sure I Break him before he moves, and trying to extend the time he stays in the Standing position from one second to three, to five, etc. If your dog tries to sit while you're trying this, move your hand farther under him and continue to move it slowly back and off him.

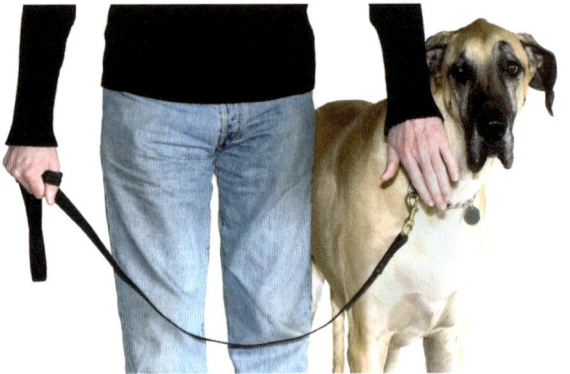

Give the verbal command and hand signal for "Stay."

Once you get him to stand with confidence for thirty seconds or more using this approach, you can move to the next step, which would be for you to stand up straight while your dog holds a stand. If he can hold his position while you're standing straight, you're ready to move to a Stand Stay. As he stands next to you, give the verbal command and hand signal you use when you leave your dog.

Back up slowly while facing your dog.

Then, just as you did when teaching him the Stay, step in front, facing him, and slowly begin to back up. Again be sure to stop and Break him before he moves.

If he looks as if he's going to move as you're backing up in front of him, use your leash hand to tug him forward and try to slide your free hand under him to keep him from sitting.

The biggest problem that occurs when teaching this command to your dog is that he may try to sit. When that happens most people get into too much of a battle getting their dogs back up into the stand position. To avoid this, try not to let your dog get all the way back into a sit. That would only make it harder for you to get him back up. Remember: to encourage him to stand when you have him in position, keep the contact with your free hand pleasurable as you slowly run the tips of your fingers across his side and off.

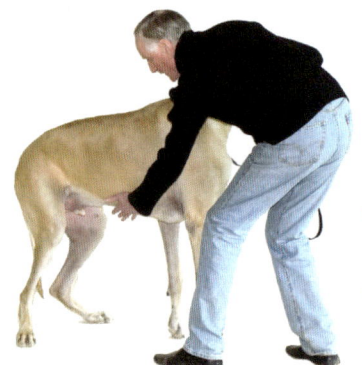

Keep him from Sitting with your free hand.

19. What should I teach my child about dogs?

Most puppies and adult dogs have a natural inclination to chase things that move. This is part of what is called their "prey drive." (See the earlier section, "Dogs are pack animals.") If you are dealing with children this is important for you to understand, because there are some simple things to remember that can prevent a dog bite from happening in the first place.

Do not let your children run around in the presence of a dog unless you know the dog well and can see that the dog is not interested in chasing. If you are approached by someone else's dog, don't be so quick to give it your hand—or your child's hand. Let the dog check you out by walking past him, and if he appears okay, pet him the next time he approaches.

If you are confronted by an uncontrolled stray, do not run. Stop and stay still until he moves on, and try to keep something between you and the dog—such as a book, a backpack, a wallet, etc. Most dogs, especially herding breeds, want to bite from behind, so be careful if you turn your back.

When your children are playing with a dog—be it their own or a friend's—encourage them to play in ways that will not provoke snapping or growling from the dog. Playing with a ball can be fine; but tug-of-war, wrestling, teasing, or playfully kicking or striking at the dog may encourage problematic dog behavior.

Tell your children to ask before petting a stranger's dog, but even then be careful. I once saw a woman with two little dogs on her lap tell two small children that it was okay to pet them. She told me later that her dogs have bitten kids in the past. I still don't understand why she would allow those children to put themselves at risk.

Do not let your children pet dogs through a fence or a car window. These places are the dog's territory and not an area to try out petting. I had one client who came out of a store to find a man holding his small child up to her car window, which was only cracked about three inches, to lift the child's arm into the car to pet her dog. This could have been a disastrous situation if the dog had felt threatened. I also have a friend who left a side slider window open on his pickup to give his German shepherd some air while he went into a store. A passing woman then went out of her way to put her hand through the window opening and got bitten by his dog. Apparently we must also protect our dogs from the ignorance of others.

20. How do you deal with aggressive dogs?

Dog–human aggression is not something everyone encounters with his or her dog, but some dogs, no matter how well they have been treated, may turn on their owner or another family member. Do you remember my sweet little poodle, Skip, mentioned at the beginning of this book? Skip was a nice dog most of the time, but when he wasn't getting his way or felt threatened, he expressed his displeasure in no uncertain terms. At those times we backed off from his growling and snarling and did what we

could to avoid provoking him. It was only fortunate that none of us got hurt, since Skip was definitely the one in control.

A situation like this can be a real problem, especially if you believe, as I do, that true obedience from your dog means he acknowledges you as his leader. As leader you should be fair and humane, and your dog should trust in you and follow your direction. If you want a pet that you can include in your life, instead of an animal you must keep isolated and/or confined, then aggression from your dog cannot be tolerated.

In my thirty-plus years as a dog trainer I've never been one to agonize too much on *why* a dog behaves as he does (aside from health or abuse issues), but to focus instead on finding a way to stop the undesirable behavior. In this way I've built my practice as a problem solver and have served many times as a "last resort" for people faced with losing their animals for uncontrollable behavior. One of the things that has made me so successful at solving biting problems is my timing. I know how long a correction should take and what to do after the correction so that the dog will understand why this (the correction) is happening. I also know what to do the next day and so on.

The method I use in dealing with aggression is a method promoted by William Koehler, formerly a dog-training instructor for the Army, and chief trainer for Walt Disney Studios. Early in my career I had the pleasure of meeting Mr. Koehler, and the very first thing I asked him was if he had found any other way of solving the problem of dogs that turn on their owners. He said, "No."

I have also been to numerous so-called "aggression seminars," to explore alternative methods. During one seminar break I asked one speaker, a well-known author, trainer, and veterinarian, "What would you do if you were teaching the Down to a German shepherd and he went for you?" I didn't get much of an answer from this gentleman, except that he would change the command to Heel and take off, thereby distracting the German shepherd from what he was trying to do.

My problem with this suggestion is that by changing what you were trying to do—teach the Down to your dog—to moving to a Heel when you can't get your dog to Down is not teaching your dog true obedience. Right at the point the dog turned, or attempted to turn on you, you had an opportunity to teach him not to threaten you. By giving up that opportunity you set yourself up for more problems down the road.

When I spot a dog getting ready to strike its handler I stop the session, take the owner into my office, and explain what will happen to the dog if it continues along this path. I show them quotes from Mr. Koehler and let them know how this method can provide rehabilitation for their dog. Over the years I've rarely had to make a strong correction. It really depends on the dog and on how serious or dangerous the situation may be. Many times I can get away with just a quick shake and move on.

So what should *you* do if you have the problem of a dog that is a protest biter? Well, to begin with, I do not think you should ignore the problem or expect it to go away with distracting treats. While you should be the one to train your dog, I think you should realize that this is a problem that

calls for professional assistance. As I mentioned, my success with this issue has much to do with my experience and my timing.

Therefore: **I do not recommend you try solving this problem without the assistance of an experienced professional.**

Could it be worth your while to get help for aggression problems? Just read one of the many letters I've received from clients who made this choice to save their dog:

Dear Ron,

I'd like to thank you for the help you gave us eleven years ago. We came to you with a two-and-a half-year-old malamute that had bitten six people. On the advice of our veterinarian we came to you as our last hope. I remember talking with my vet before we took that step. He was very blunt with me. He told me to trust you; he explained how my dog could not be hurt (other than the short term discomfort) and he reminded me that if our training failed our only alternative would be to put her to sleep. It was a tough decision, but we trusted your judgment and it worked. Our dog lived ten more years, never biting again. We could take her with us anywhere and enjoyed her as part of the family. I don't know if I can ever express my thanks enough. If sharing this letter will help anyone who may be in a similar situation, please feel free to use it. As we have learned, overly aggressive dogs can be trained to live as a member of the family. Thanks so much!
T. & L. Farrow

Afterword

Along with a training technique, I hope this book will leave you with an understanding of the following important points:

- Good training does not involve hitting, yelling, or otherwise abusing animals.
- Training is a process. You must first build a bridge of communication with your pet before you can hope to make effective commands or corrections.
- There is a learning phase and a correction phase. First show your dog what you want of him, then correct his mistakes.
- When you end a correction is as important as when you start one: your body language clarifies to your dog what behavior you want from him.
- You are your dog's leader. Always strive to be fair and consistent.

Acknowledgments

The authors wish to express their thanks and appreciation to the following people and pets for their significant contributions to this book:

Lars Commes – for his technical support
Russ Carmack – for his photography illustrating training maneuvers
Bev Sparks – for her dog photography
Ryan Moss – for his photographic adjustments
Lisa Anderson – for her editing

Janet Hersey and Cinder – for demonstrating leash handling
Kyan – for helping Ron show the leash correction for jumping
Patti Pace and Jay for demonstrating the Triangle Exercise
Kary Fugal and Moses – for their demonstration of Heel
Pepper – who helped demonstrate the leash position for Heel
Justina Pace Riippi and Riley – for their demonstration of Stay
Spencer Sproul and Coco – for their demonstration of on-leash Come
Kelly Reiten and Squints – for their demonstration of the Finish
Jill Lensegrav and Jayda – for their demonstration of Down
Ben Riippi and Daisy – for showing the Don't Touch command
Cheri Carlson and Viggo – for showing the Drop command
Kim Shea and Zeus – for demonstrating the Patrol position
Ray Shea – for posing as an approaching stranger for the chapter on Patrol
Travis Gimse and Champ – for demonstrating off-leash Come
Jarod Pace and Captain – for demonstrating the Stay Back command
Alek Jackson – for posing as a distraction for Captain
Jarod Pace and Rocco – for demonstrating the car as a permanent boundary
Cara Putnam and Simon – for illustrating how to handle the distraction of another dog
Janet Hersey and Tawney – for providing the distraction of another dog in that lesson
Cara Putnam and Daisy – for showing how to correct digging
Cara Putnam and Bandit – for showing the correction off furniture
Jazz – for acting as an approaching dog in photograph showing how to deter other dogs
Timothy Thomas and Clark – for demonstrating the Stand

Index

age. *See* dog's readiness for training.
aggression, 23, 30, 145-146, 161, 163, 165-167
anger, 24, 151
Automatic Sit, 57-60
   correction for not sitting straight, 59
   holding the position, 60
balancing the correction, 33, 45, 104
barking, correction for, 154-156
   in car, 156
barking, reasons for, 154
   for a good reason, 155, 156
biting the leash, correction for, 44
"board and train" method, 16, 17, 18, 26-27
body language, your dog's, 23, 24, 129
boundary, permanent, 135-140
   car, 135-138
   property lines, 139-140
boundary, temporary, 31, 127-128
   teaching, 128-132
"Break" command, 47
brick wall effect, 48, 50, 56
car, as permanent boundary. *See* boundary, permanent, car.
car, barking in, 156
cat, 162
chain, choke. *See* collar, choke.
children and dogs, 161, 165
classical conditioning, 25
clicker training, 25
collar, choke, 35, 37
   proper way to put on, 38-39
   selecting a size, 38
collar, electronic, 160-161
collar, metal, 35, 38
collar, nylon, 36
collar, pinch. *See* collar, prong.

collar, prong, 39, 156
commands, 24, 31, 47, 54, 69, 70, 78, 83, 84, 85, 86, 89, 90, 96, 99, 100, 101, 103, 104, 107, 121, 128
Come, 30, 77-78, 79, 119
   if dog does not Come, 122-123
   off-leash Come, 119, 121-123
   on-leash Come, 30, 77-78
communication, importance of, 21
conditioned stimulus, 25
contact with other dogs, 144, 159-160, 163
contact with other people, 112
control issues, 22
correction phase, 31, 59
corrections, 24, 31, 33
   Also see balancing the correction.
distraction, of another dog, 31, 143
distractions, avoiding, 30, 50, 90
distractions, introducing, 75, 132, 139
dog run. *See* kennel.
dog's readiness for training, 29-30
"Don't Touch," 31, 103, 150, 152, 158, 161, 162
   other dogs as a permanent Don't Touch, 143
   overriding a permanent Don't Touch, 106-107
   permanent, 105
   temporary, 105
   what it means, 103
Down, 30, 89-101
   challenges of teaching, 90
   first technique for teaching, 91-92
   from the front, 99-101
   from the side, 89
   getting up from the Down, 95
   inching forward during Down, 95

   practicing, 94
   problems you may encounter, 95
   second technique for teaching, 92
   sniffing the ground during Down, 95-96
   teaching the Down, 90-96, 99-101
   third technique for teaching, 92-93
   value of, 90
"Down" command, what it means, 89-90
"Drop," 107-108
emotions, 150, 157
eye contact, 46-47
Finish, 30, 83-86
   Finish from Break, 84-85
   Finish from sit-in-front, 86
   things to remember, 86
   what it means, 83
food-based training, 25
frequency of practice, 30-31, 61, 94
hand praise, 32, 60
hand signals, 78, 79, 84, 86, 91, 96, 99, 100, 101, 121, 128, 163-164
health. *See* dog's readiness for training.
Heel, 30, 50, 53-57, 61, 63-66, 83-84, 85, 86, 111
   changing your pace while Heeling, 65-66
   correction for bolting ahead, 64, 66
   correction for lagging behind, 64, 66
   leash position for, 54
"Heel" command, what it means, 54, 83-85
Heel position, 70, 73, 74, 83
injuries, preventing, 9
jumping up, on doors, 158-159
jumping up, on others, 24, 46, 138-139
jumping up, on you, 44

kennel, 38, 124, 153
  dog-friendly, 153
  safe, 153
  standard size, 154
Koehler, William (Bill), 13, 166
learning phase, 24, 31, 59, 128
leash, 35
  biting the leash, 44
  holding the leash, 36
  introducing dog to the leash, 36-37
  retractable, 36
  snapping vs. pulling, 44, 45, 46, 49, 56
  thickness and width, 36
  using to establish leadership, 43
leash angles, 53, 59, 60, 61, 72, 79, 92
Left Turn, 65
Left–About Turn, 65
let go. See "Drop."
"Make Friends," 112, 159
negative reinforcement, 31
on Break, 47
other dogs, encountering, 144-146
  Also see contact with other dogs; distraction, of another dog; "Don't Touch," other dogs as a permanent Don't Touch.
"Out!" 154
overcorrection, 23, 33, 160
pack instincts, 23, 24, 26, 156
pack leader, 23, 24
pat on the back, 33, 45
  different from praise, 32
Patrol position, 111
  advantages of, 111
  vs. Heel, 113
permanent boundary. *See* boundary, permanent.

permanent "Don't Touch." *See* "Don't Touch," permanent.
positive reinforcement, 31
practicing, frequency, 30-31, 61, 94
praise, 23, 31
  Also see verbal praise; hand praise.
pulling too hard on leash, correction for, 48
puppies, 25, 36, 37
  Also see dog's readiness for training.
"Quiet!" 154
"read" your dog, 23, 53, 61, 66
"return to your dog," 73-74
Right–About Turn, 60-61
Right Turns, 55
"rubbing him up," 32
safety, 9, 90, 140, 154
second dog, 163
sensitive dogs, 33
side step, 63-64
  side step back, 64
  side step forward, 65
  to the side, 63
Sit, 86, 96, 101, 121, 123
  from the Down, 96
  from the front, 101
  from the side, 96
  Also see Automatic Sit.
sit-in-front, 78-79, 80
Sit/Stay, 70-72
slack leash, 36, 37, 44, 47, 50, 54, 58, 61, 71, 78, 100, 113
"Stand," 163-164
Stand Stay, 164
Stay, 30, 69-75
  leaving your dog on a Stay, 70-72
"Stay Back," 128-133
  from a distance, 133
  practicing, 132

"Stay" command, what it means, 69, 127
tab, 120
"Take It," 107, 153
temperament, 32
temporary boundary. *See* boundary, temporary.
temporary "Don't Touch." *See* "Don't Touch," temporary.
throw chains, 121, 122
time frame for training process, 30-31
training area, optimum, 50, 90
training process, 29
treats, as training incentive, 25
triangle exercise, 49-51
undercorrection, 33
verbal praise, 32
walking on Break, 47
yelling, 151
younger dogs, 29-30

CPSIA information can be obtained at www.ICGtesting.com
Printed in the USA
BVIW12n1758181015
422401BV00004B/14